To Max, who particularly likes trees to hide behind.

A History of Trees

Simon Wills

WHITE
OWL

First published in Great Britain in 2018 by
Pen & Sword White Owl
an imprint of
Pen & Sword Books Ltd
47 Church Street
Barnsley
South Yorkshire
S70 2AS

ISBN 978 1 52670 159 6

Typeset in Ehrhardt by
Mac Style
Printed and bound by Replika Press Pvt. Ltd., India

Pen & Sword Books Limited incorporates the imprints of Atlas, Archaeology, Aviation, Discovery, Family History, Fiction, History, Maritime, Military, Military Classics, Politics, Select, Transport, True Crime, Air World, Frontline Publishing, Leo Cooper, Remember When, Seaforth Publishing, The Praetorian Press, Wharncliffe Local History, Wharncliffe Transport, Wharncliffe True Crime and White Owl.

For a complete list of Pen & Sword titles please contact
PEN & SWORD BOOKS LIMITED
47 Church Street, Barnsley, South Yorkshire, S70 2AS, England
E-mail: enquiries@pen-and-sword.co.uk
Website: www.pen-and-sword.co.uk

Contents

Introduction   vi
Acknowledgements   viii

Alder   1
Apple   6
Ash   15
Bay   23
Beech   30
Birch   38
Cherry   44
Elm   52
Hawthorn   62
Hazel   71
Holly   78
Hornbeam   85
Horse Chestnut   91
Lime   95
London Plane   102
Magnolia   107
Maple   112
Monkey Puzzle   118
Oak   123
Pear   135
Pine   141
Poplar   148
Rowan   156
Sweet Chestnut   162
Sycamore   169
Walnut   176
Willow   181
Yew   192

Index   202

Introduction

*T*rees and woodland have perhaps always had a special place in our psyche, maybe because we are apes and we know that we 'came from the trees'. My interest in trees started as a child. My parents loved Badbury Rings in Dorset with its famous huge double avenue of beech trees, so we often went there, and I still think it's wonderful. I was a determined tree climber too, and still have the wrist injury that resulted from a fall sustained about forty years ago.

Trees impress us because of their size, majesty, beauty and endurance. Many of them live to a greater age than we do, so it is possible to sit next to an elderly oak tree and ponder that it was standing throughout the reign of Queen Anne and when Nelson won at Trafalgar. And plenty of trees have witnessed even greater spans of history than this.

Trees also connect us with nature: they demonstrate the seasons very dramatically in the case of deciduous trees, they provide homes and food for multiple other organisms, and they are very visible and characteristic features of British gardens, parks, towns and countryside. In earlier centuries, when the countryside was bigger and more people lived and worked in it, the practical benefits of trees to everyday life were both more numerous and more obvious. Trees provided our ancestors with food, timber for construction, medicines, protection from the elements, boundary markers, creative inspiration, fuel, charcoal and folklore. One of our favourite national heroes, Robin Hood, lived in a forest, and certain trees were held to be sacred to the ancient druids or were believed to be inhabited by spirits and elves.

As a lover of trees, it has been difficult to decide which trees to include and which to leave out. The choice is to some extent dictated by the size of the book, which makes it impossible to include every British tree. However, I have tried to focus on trees that have an interesting tale to tell, and are common and familiar. Within the text I have, from time to time, described certain trees as being 'native' and perhaps this term needs some explanation. Trees described as native are the ones that grew in the UK after the end of the last ice age while this country was still physically connected to mainland Europe; non-native trees are those that were brought here by humans at a later date. I have used the categorisation of native species promoted by the Woodland Trust (www. woodlandtrust.org.uk) as the basis for my use of this term.

Beyond their practical utility to us and our simple liking of them, trees form the great forests of the world, which are said to be the lungs of the planet. So trees, more than anything else, keep us alive.

Acknowledgements

Many websites now make original historical texts available freely to researchers and historians, and I would like to take this opportunity to thank them, and especially the following:

Complete Works of William Shakespeare: http://shakespeare.mit.edu/
Internet Archive: https://archive.org/
Early English Books Online: http://quod.lib.umich.edu/e/eebogroup/
Google Books: https://books.google.co.uk/
Perseus Digital Library: http://www.perseus.tufts.edu/hopper/
Project Gutenberg: http://www.gutenberg.org/

Note that where I have quoted from some of the more ancient authors, I have sometimes altered spellings and punctuation to match modern English usage.

I am particularly grateful that two organisations allow writers to use illustrations from their priceless online collections for research and for publication:

British Library illuminated manuscripts: www.bl.uk/catalogues/illuminatedmanuscripts uses a Creative Commons Public Domain Dedication https://www.bl.uk/catalogues/illuminatedmanuscripts/reuse.asp

The Wellcome Collection https://wellcomecollection.org also makes many images available under a Creative Commons licence https://creativecommons.org/licenses/by/4.0/

Jeanie Smith and the staff at the Guildhall Library in London kindly helped me with access to some resources, as did the staff of the Royal Pharmaceutical Society Library. Thank you.

My editor Linne Matthews has been brilliant as ever and I wanted to thank her for being so careful and thorough, and lovely with it. My partner, B, is always caring and supportive, but especially when I am writing a book: I don't know what I'd do without him. Anyone who has a writer in the house will know what I'm saying here. Finally, I would like to thank Max, to whom this book is dedicated, for allowing me to frequently stop his walk and take photos of trees. He's very tolerant.

Alder

Distinctive leaves of
common alder.

*A*lder or 'aller' was a valuable tree to our ancestors. All parts of it were exploited to make dyes, including the leaves, bark, wood, catkins and twigs, and they produced a variety of colours – yellow, green, brown, black and red – depending upon the dyeing technique. Sixteenth-century herbalist John Gerard explained that 'the bark is much used of poor country dyers for the dying of coarse cloth, caps, hose and such like into a black colour, whereto it serveth very well.' The dried catkins were used to make an ink, and the astringent alder bark was sometimes employed in the leather industry for tanning.

The tree grows mainly in damp conditions – the seventeenth-century writer John Evelyn described it as 'the most faithful lover of water and boggy places'. When freshly cut, the timber has a characteristic bright orange colour, and although not as extensively used as many other woods, alder has some useful properties. It was soon discovered, for example, that the timber itself was particularly suited to wet conditions where it could retain its integrity for long periods. Neolithic people in the UK are known to have laid down alder logs to support raised structures in the water such as jetties. In the west of England, a Neolithic walkway known as Abbot's Way was constructed to cross the boggy Somerset Levels in safety. Just over 2.5 kilometres long, it joined the sand island of Burtle with the rock island of Westhay and comprises over 30,000 split alder logs or planks.

Dried catkins of alder were used to make dyes and ink; the seeds they contain are also an important source of winter food for birds such as siskins.

When recently felled, alder timber is bright orange.

Roman writers such as Virgil and Lucan record the use of alder for building boats and the city of Ravenna was raised out of the marshy lagoon it inhabited by the use of alder wood piles. Similarly, large parts of Venice are still built on alder timbers, which were driven down beneath the water through soft muddy sediments and into the harder clay underneath the city. In the Netherlands, alder has long been found suitable for constructing the piles for bridges and dykes. An English translation of a sixteenth-century French work, *Maison Rustique*, records prevailing European views about the value of alder as a building material:

> The aller or alder tree…doth serve…to lay the foundations of buildings upon, which are laide in the rivers, fennes or other standing waters, because it never rotteth in the water, but lasteth as it were for ever.

In the UK, the roots of alder trees have provided valuable support to river banks by protecting them from erosion and were sometimes deliberately planted there for this purpose; the timber was also chosen for constructing piles to shore up unstable riverbanks. The durability of the wood when wet made alder ideal for manufacturing the barrels needed by the herring industry, especially in Scotland, where one author commented that whole meadows were regularly denuded every year of this type of timber. Alder was used for pit props in damp mine workings, for roofing, and even hollowed out to create wooden pipes to conduct water – something that was regular practice well into the

A mature alder growing by a river: its ideal location. This tree has been coppiced in the past, perhaps to provide wood for charcoal manufacture.

Scottish fisher girls in about 1890 processing herrings – the barrels to store them were commonly made of alder because it could withstand being wet for long periods.

nineteenth century. In addition, compared to many other timbers, alder is less inclined to split, so it could be carved into comparatively long-lasting wooden clogs or handles for tools.

Alder was one of many trees that were coppiced in order to make charcoal, but alder charcoal was accorded the honour of producing the finest domestic charcoal for the production of gunpowder, so it was much in demand. In the eighteenth and nineteenth centuries, the proprietors of gunpowder factories in Hounslow, London were so anxious to ensure that they had sufficient ongoing supplies that they maintained large plantations of alder, which were coppiced every five to six years.

Alder had a number of purported medicinal uses. John Gerard explained that in Tudor times, 'the leaves of alder are much used against hot swellings, ulcers, and all inward inflammations, especially of the almonds and kernels of the throat.' Almonds and kernels here refer to the tonsils and glands. Nicholas Culpeper recounts varied additional uses for alder leaves:

The fresh leaves laid upon swellings dissolveth them, and stayeth the inflammations; the leaves put under the bare feet galled with travelling are a great refreshing to them; the said leaves gathered while the morning dew is on them and brought into a chamber troubled with fleas, will gather them thereinto [and] being suddenly cast out will rid the chamber of those troublesome bed-fellows.

In addition, alder beaten into vinegar was said to cure 'the itch', which probably referred to skin infestation with things like lice, fleas and mites.

Apple

*T*he UK is a cold and wet place, which was not entirely conducive to the growing of many varieties of fruit in Anglo-Saxon times. So it is not surprising to learn that the word 'apple' may originally have been a generic word for any kind of fruit growing on a tree. After all, in northern Europe there were not many to choose from. However, as other types of tree fruit became more well known, the term 'apple' was confined to one particular kind of fruit.

The apple tree was probably the first tree to be deliberately grown by humans to produce food. The cultivated apple has the scientific name *Malus pumila*, although it is sometimes also called *Malus domestica*. It is not native to the UK or Europe, and seems to have originated in Asia, where its principal wild ancestor, the Central Asian wild apple (*Malus sieversii*), can still be found. This Asian species was selectively bred by humans to eventually create a new species – the cultivated apple – between 4,000 and 10,000 years ago. As this tree began growing further and further from its original home it acquired additional genetic input from other apple species by hybridisation, including the European wild crab apple (*Malus sylvestris*), often called the 'wilding' in the past.

Apple blossom.

Today there are over 7,500 varieties of apple around the globe, and it is probably the most common fruit in the world.

A big advantage that apples have over other commonly grown fruits is that they can be carefully stored whole and may last for months without the need for preservation. This was a valuable distinction in the past, when fruit such as cherries, plums and pears had to be eaten within a few days of being picked or they would rot. Apples were so important that some people specialised in selling them. The old-fashioned term 'costermonger' conventionally referred to a street seller of fresh fruit and vegetables, and sometimes other items. Yet in Tudor times the original version of this word was a 'costard-monger', who sold only apples – the costard being a popular large variety of apple.

The commonness and importance of apples is reflected in the ways in which they feature so often in our language. For example, a man's voice box is his Adam's apple; someone who is a bad influence is called a rotten apple; there is a colour known as apple white; New York is The Big Apple; the phrase 'apples and pears' was once Cockney rhyming slang for stairs, and so forth. In addition there are many idioms and proverbs involving the apple: an apple a day keeps the doctor away; as sure as God made little apples; one bad apple spoils the barrel; the apple never falls far from the tree, and many more. One of the most common is the phrase 'the apple of my eye'. This phrase dates back to the early medieval period and arose because the iris was once thought to be a dark orb floating within the eye. Since the iris was believed to have a similar shape to a tiny apple and eyesight was so precious, the phrase 'apple of my eye' came to mean someone highly treasured.

Adam and Eve, each with an apple, and accompanied by the evil snake coiled around the tree of knowledge. From the fourteenth-century *Taymouth Hours*. (*Courtesy of the British Library illuminated manuscripts collection www.bl.uk*)

The apple was at the centre of certain superstitions too. One old ritual was to throw the peel of an apple over the head: if it remained whole you would soon be married; if it broke you were to remain single. A similar custom was that the coiled apple peel would reveal the initial of the next person you would fall in love with.

Apples feature prominently in well-known stories of various kinds. The wicked queen gave Snow White a poisoned apple; rivalry between three Greek goddesses over a golden apple triggered the Trojan War; William Tell shot an apple off his son's head with a crossbow; one of the twelve trials of Hercules was to steal some of Zeus's golden apples from his secret garden. However, undoubtedly the most famous of all these mythical tales is the story of Adam and Eve. The snake in the Garden of Eden encouraged Eve to tempt Adam to eat the fruit from the 'tree of knowledge of good and evil'. This went against God's express instructions, and as a result the couple were evicted from paradise. The actual fruit is not specified in the Bible, but longstanding tradition dating back to the earliest centuries of Christianity has represented the tree as an apple tree. This choice was probably made simply because apples were a common fruit in Europe, but it may have been influenced by the fact that the Latin word *malus* can mean both apple and evil.

A tale that seems to have at least some element of truth is the famous story of Isaac Newton and the apple. According to convention, the young Newton was inspired to create a theory about gravity when he saw an apple fall to the ground from a tree in his mother's garden in Woolsthorpe, Lincolnshire. It's a story that he may have embellished over time, but in 1726, a young colleague, William Stukeley, gave this account of a discussion he had with Newton, then an old man, about the event in question:

After dinner, the weather being warm, we went into the garden and drank thea [= tea] under the shade of some apple tree; only he and myself. Amid other discourse, he told me, he was just in the same situation, as when formerly the notion of gravitation came into his mind. Why sh[oul]d that apple always descend perpendicularly to the ground, thought he to himself; occasion'd by the fall of an apple, as he sat in contemplative mood.

Why sh[oul]d it not go sideways, or upwards? But constantly to the Earth's centre? Assuredly the reason is, that the Earth draws it. There must be a drawing power in matter. And the sum of the drawing power in the matter of the Earth must be in the Earth's centre, not in any side of the Earth.

Therefore does this apple fall perpendicularly or towards the centre? If matter thus draws matter; it must be proportion of its quantity. Therefore the apple draws the Earth, as well as the Earth draws the apple.

More recently, another famous British scientist has been associated with an apple, but unfortunately for tragic reasons. Alan Turing, the pioneer wartime computer scientist of Bletchley Park fame, was found dead in 1954. The coroner concluded that he had committed suicide with cyanide, which was found on the premises and may have been

Alan Turing
memorial
statue in
Manchester
with an
apple on his
knee.

The cider drinker's lament

Particular types of apple such as 'redstreak' and 'sline' were traditionally grown to yield the juice that was fermented to make cider. Some areas of the country became famous for their cider – especially Herefordshire, Worcestershire, Somerset and Devon – and cider production was a popular cottage industry in the Tudor and Stuart periods. Yet it had a dark side.

'Devonshire colic' was a longstanding and mysterious disease of the West Country. Victims suffered from painful abdominal cramps, became very pale, and then sank into a stupor before dying. It affected men more than women. It wasn't until the eighteenth century that it was shown to be an affliction confined exclusively to people who drank cider. The cause was eventually revealed as lead poisoning. The apple juice used to make the cider was so acidic that it gradually dissolved the metal of the fermentation equipment employed by many small-scale producers, and so the victims were in fact drinking a highly toxic solution of lead salts.

ingested by eating an apple laced with it, as an apple was found by his body. A criminal conviction for homosexual behaviour had possibly contributed to this sorrowful end to a great man's life.

The popularity of apples in the UK has meant that the country has always had to import some to meet demand. Even in the 1820s, the UK imported an estimated 20,000

The Cox is a well-known British variety of apple.

bushels of apples from France and the USA. France has been an important influencer of apple production in the UK, and many earlier varieties were imports from there.

However, the UK has produced many apple varieties of its own. The most well-known eating apple from the these shores is Cox's orange pippin, originally grown by horticulturalist Richard Cox at Colnbrook, Buckinghamshire in 1830. The Cox is an important apple in UK fruit history because so many other varieties are descended from it (e.g. Laxton superb, fiesta). It is also the most widely grown dessert apple in the UK.

One of the most famous cooking apples in the world is another UK variety, Bramley. This was grown from seed by a young girl named Mary Anne Brailsford in her garden at Southwell, Nottinghamshire, between 1809 and 1815, but it did not produce apples until 1837. At some point after this, the tree's delicious cooked fruit came to the attention of a gardener named Henry Merryweather who sought permission from the new owner of the house to take cuttings from the tree in order to sell them. The householder, Matthew Bramley, was happy to oblige and the variety was named after him. Other UK apple varieties include discovery, egremont russet, Worcester pearmain and Blenheim orange.

In recent years, some of the most popular apples sold in the UK have originated from New Zealand (braeburn, gala, jazz), the US (golden delicious, jonagold, enterprise), and from Australia (Granny Smith, pink lady). Granny Smith was named after a real person. In the 1860s, Maria Ann Smith from New South Wales threw out into her yard some old apple waste, and one of the pips germinated. The apples from the tree were an unusually bright green, had a good taste, could be cooked or eaten raw, and stored remarkably well. So, she started selling them. Mrs Smith was by then a grandmother and 'Granny Smith's' apples sold in large numbers. As a result, everyone wanted to grow their own and they were soon planted commercially, eventually becoming a worldwide bestseller.

Orchards were special places in a farming community because they provided food that would last over winter, and picking the apples was a source of employment. Perhaps understandably, our ancestors had all sorts of superstitions about orchards: for example, that spirits dwelled amongst the trees and had to be appeased to ensure a good crop. The habit of wassailing in orchards is one variation on this theme. It seems to have been especially common in the West Country. Groups of local people would enter the orchard at a particular time of the year, often around the date of Twelfth Night, and sing an incantation to exhort the trees to bear good fruit. One example is:

> Here's to thee, old apple-tree,
> Whence thou may'st bud, and whence thou may'st blow;
> And whence thou may'st bear apples enow.
> Hats full! Caps full!
> Bushel, bushel, sacks full!
> And my pockets full, too!
> Huzza! Huzza!

Landowner and worker in an orchard, featured in a translation of *Ruralia Commoda* by Pietro Crescenzi published about 1480. (*Courtesy of the British Library illuminated manuscripts collection www.bl.uk*)

This chanting was variously accompanied by blowing horns or shouting to scare bad spirits away, libations of cider on selected trees as an offering, dancing around trees, or hanging tokens from the trees' branches.

To apples were attributed a number of surprising medicinal properties. The well-known seventeenth-century herbalist Nicholas Culpeper notes that 'Roasted apples are good for the asthmatic; either raw, roasted or boiled are good for the consumptive [TB sufferer], in inflammations of the breasts or lungs.' However, the Tudor herbalist John Gerard describes a quite staggering array of uses for

Victorian image of young boys 'scrumping' for apples: not everyone who took apples from an orchard was entitled to them and there was the danger of getting caught… (*Courtesy of Wellcome Collection https://wellcomecollection.org*)

the humble apple. He says they are valuable for treating a weak stomach and could be applied to sites of inflammation, but then adds some rather surprising properties:

> The juice of apples which be sweet and of a middle taste is mixed in compositions of diverse medicines, and also for the tempering of melancholy humours [i.e. treating depression]…
>
> There is likewise made an ointment with the pulp of apples and swines' grease [= lard] and rosewater, which is used to beautify the face, and to take away the roughness of the skin, which is called in shops 'Pomatum'…
>
> The pulp of the roasted apples, in number four or five according to the greatness of the apples…mixed in a wine quart of fair water, laboured together until it come to be as apples and ale (which we call 'lambs wool') and the whole quart drunk last at night, within the space of an hour doth in one night cure those that piss by drops with great anguish and dolour, the stranguary, and all other diseases proceeding of the difficulty of making water. But in twice taking, it never faileth in any. Oftentimes there happeneth with the aforesaid diseases, the gonorrhoea, or running of the rains, which it likewise healeth in those persons, but not generally in all…
>
> Apples cut in pieces, and distilled with a quantity of camphite and butter-milk, take away the marks and scars gotten by the smallpox, being washed therewith when they grow unto their state and ripeness: provided that you give unto the patient a little milk and saffron, or milk and mithridate [= an antidote to poison], to drink to expel to the extreme parts that venom which may lie hid and as yet not seen.

So there you have it: no wonder that an apple a day keeps the doctor away.

Ash

Ash seeds or 'keys'.

*T*he ancient Greeks believed that ash trees were important enough to be the homes of specific nature deities called the Meliae. These nymphs of the forest brought up the father of the gods, Zeus, when he was a baby, and helped him create the first humans of the Bronze Age out of ash timber.

The Yggdrasil tree with the three young virgins known as Norns; the eagle, squirrel and serpent were also integral parts of the Norse legend.

The ash tree was even more important in Norse mythology. The nineteenth-century writer Thomas Carlyle was particularly interested in this subject and described the ancient beliefs of the Scandinavians:

> All life is figured by them as a tree. Igdrasil, the ash tree of existence, has its roots deep down in the kingdoms of Hela or Death; its trunk reaches up heaven-high, spreads its boughs over the whole universe: it is the Tree of Existence. At the foot of it, in the Death-kingdom, sit three Nornas, fates – the Past, Present, Future; watering its roots from the Sacred Well. Its 'boughs' with their buddings and disleafings [are] events, things suffered, things done, catastrophes – [and] stretch through all lands and times. Is not every leaf of it a biography…?

This ash tree was so immense that it reached to heaven, and the Norse gods such as Odin, Thor and Loki held court beneath it every day. It is more usually denoted Yggdrasil and the three maidens beneath it were the Norns called Urd ('fate'), Skuld ('being') and Verandi ('necessity'). According to the Old Norse poems known as the Edda, an eagle resided at the top of the ash tree to observe the world. A squirrel lived in the tree as well, and served to alert the eagle to anything that he might have missed, and there was a serpent that gnawed the tree's roots. Two streams flowed from the base of Yggdrasil: one contained knowledge and the other knew the future. In some forms of the legend, the first man, Ask, was formed from the wood of the ash tree by Odin.

Perhaps it is the remembrance of these important pagan beliefs that has lent the ash tree so many superstitious associations in the UK and elsewhere. From the earliest times, the ash has been acclaimed as an antidote to sorcery, and a defence against the black arts and evil spirits. In the Highlands of Scotland the juice of an ash twig was customarily the first drink given to newborn babies in order to protect them from harm. Ash has long been a favourite wood for walking sticks, seemingly because it is particularly well suited to the purpose, but the protective powers of the tree were also valuable to the walker in case he was suddenly confronted by evil.

Ancient writers attested to the ability of ash to defy snakes and even in the sixteenth century this was still believed. Pliny may have been the first to make this claim, and says of the ash tree:

> So great, too, are the virtues of this tree, that no serpent will ever lie in the shadow thrown by it, either in the morning or the evening, be it ever so long; indeed, they will always keep at the greatest possible distance from it. We state the fact from visual observation, that if a serpent and a lighted fire are placed within a circle formed of the leaves of the ash, the reptile will rather throw itself into the fire than encounter the leaves of the tree.

Interestingly, although Tudor herbalist John Gerard faithfully reported these words of Pliny, and so by implication believed them, around fifty years later Nicholas Culpeper

Mature ash tree in leaf.

stated that this was all nonsense. He did, however, endorse the opinion of the ancient Greek physician Dioscorides, that ash leaves in wine were a cure for snake bites.

There were a whole host of very odd behaviours involving the ash tree in England. It was well-established practice to split a living young ash tree down the middle and pass a child with a hernia through the gap to cure it. The ruptured tree was nailed up afterwards and as the tree healed so did the child, supposedly. Even stranger was the custom of boring a hole in an ash tree to imprison an unfortunate shrew. Branches taken from this tree were then used to strike cattle to cure them of lameness, which was said to be caused by shrews.

The leaves of the ash have attracted attention because of their elegant pinnate shape, and the fact that the ash tree, like the oak, is one of the later trees to come into leaf. This led to much folklore speculation as to whether the relative timing of the leaves' appearance was a prognosticator for the weather forecast. There are many variations on this theme, but a popular one was the rhyme 'Ash before oak we're in for a soak; oak before ash we're in for a splash.' This suggests that if the ash comes into leaf first then it will be a wet summer, but if oak produces leaves first then there will only be a splash of rain – in other words, a dry summer. It's a charming tradition, but sadly weather records clearly show this old adage is not correct. Ash leaves were also sometimes an autumn feed for cattle if other fodder was scarce, but there was a diversity of opinion about whether this was appropriate for dairy cows. Some held that eating ash leaves would turn the milk rank, and any butter produced from it would not be fit to be eaten, hence many dairy farmers refused to allow ash trees to grow on grazing land.

The enchanted properties of ash probably encouraged people to believe that it should have healing properties, and a great number of medicinal virtues were ascribed to it. This seems to have been true even in Anglo-Saxon times, where one recorded cure for deafness featured the ash:

> Take a green stick of ash, lay it over a fire, then take the juice which comes out, put it in wool, wring it into the ear and stop up the ear with the same wool.

Generally, the leaves were taken medicinally in preference, but the bark was as an alternative if the leaves were not yet in season. Ash was used to treat dropsy, a build-up of fluid often caused by conditions such as heart failure or kidney disease that doctors

The distinctive pinnate leaves of the ash. It is one of the later trees to produce its leaves, but also one of the earliest to shed them all.

Ash bark is often attractively patterned with lichens, moss and fissures. Like the leaves, it was used medicinally in the past.

nowadays call oedema. It was recommended for gangrene and kidney stones, and made into a tonic as well – a kind of universal pick-me-up. An oil extracted from the wood was accounted valuable to treat deafness, 'rot of the bones', toothache and other pains.

The ash tree was supposed to be able to remove warts as well. There were various methods advocated for this, but in one version a person would cross each wart with a pin three times then say this rhyme after each crossing: 'Ash tree, ashen tree: pray buy this wart of me!' The pin was then stuck in the tree and left there. The wart would soon disappear and grow on the tree instead.

John Gerard, describes some of the other remedies that could be made from ash:

Both the leaves and the bark are reported to stop the belly, and being boiled with vinegar and water do stay vomiting, if they be laid upon the stomach. The leaves and bark of the ash tree boiled in wine and drunk, do open stoppings of the liver and spleen, and do greatly comfort them. Three or four leaves of the ash tree taken in wine each morning from time to time, do make those lean that are fat, and keep them from feeding that begin to wax fat.

The seeds of the ash tree are produced in large clusters and have a passing likeness perhaps to a bunch of keys, and have long been called 'ash keys'. The Romans as well as European apothecaries knew them as *lingua avis* or 'bird's tongue' because of some supposed resemblance between the two. Gerard says they were helpful to 'provoke urine, increase natural seed [male fertility], and stir up bodily lust especially being powdered with nutmegs and drunk'. In former times, the new green seeds were pickled to eat as a salad, or to produce a sauce. It was a dire portent if ash trees produced no keys and great danger would face the nation; in many versions of this superstition the prophecy was the imminent death of the monarch.

The wood of the ash tree was much valued because it was strong. Many historical writers noted that only oak was in greater demand. In fact it was known as the 'husbandman's tree' because its timber was so commonly taken to make good quality agricultural implements, poles, pulleys, walking sticks, ladders, handles for tools and axes, buckets, crates, and a great many other practical everyday items. It was also used to construct larger objects that needed to withstand wear and tear such as wheels, oars, kitchen tables, the beams of ploughs, and even staircases. Ash has been a favourite for sporting equipment such as the stumps and bails in cricket, tennis rackets and hockey sticks. It had military uses too – traditionally being crafted to form the hafts of spears and pikes, and as a second-best substitute for yew in making the bows that shot the archer's arrows. John Evelyn described the universal use of ash with great enthusiasm:

So useful and profitable is this tree (next to the oak) that every prudent lord of a manor should employ one acre of ground with ash or acorns to every 20 acres of land; since in as many years, it would be worth more than the land itself.

Wood from a recently felled ash – it has a characteristic pale colour, almost white.

Methodist family tree

The ash does not live to a very great age, so there are few individual trees that have attracted specific names. However, an exception is the Wesley Tree at Winchelsea in Sussex. Here in 1790, Methodist theologian John Wesley preached his last open-air sermon to a large crowd. In his journal, Wesley recalled the event: 'I stood under a large tree and called to most of the inhabitants of the town "the kingdom of heaven is at hand"…' Unfortunately, this tree was blown down in 1927, but the tree now growing in its place was created from a cutting of the original.

Bay

Bay leaves ready for cooking.

*T*he bay tree or bay laurel had a special place in Greek mythology and culture. According to legend, the water nymph Daphne, daughter of a river god, was very beautiful and Apollo lusted after her. He pursued her and, desperate to save her virtue, she cried out for help. Her father quickly transformed his frightened daughter into the first bay tree, as described poetically by Ovid in his appropriately titled *Metamorphoses*:

> A heavy torpor seizes her limbs; and her soft breasts are covered with a thin bark. Her hair grows into green leaves, her arms into branches; her feet, the moment before so swift, adhere by sluggish roots; a leafy canopy overspreads her features; her elegance alone remains in her. This, too, Phœbus [= Apollo] admires, and placing his right hand upon the stock, he perceives that the breast still throbs

Detail of a miniature of Daphne, the nymph who was turned into a bay tree while fleeing from Apollo, in *The Book of the Queen*, Paris, 1410–14. *(Courtesy of the British Library illuminated manuscripts collection www.bl.uk)*

beneath the new bark; and then, embracing the branches as though limbs in his arms, he gives kisses to the wood, and yet the wood shrinks from his kisses. To her the god said: 'But since you cannot be my wife, at least you will be my tree: my hair, my lyre, my quiver shall always be yours, oh laurel! You will be presented to Roman leaders when the joyous voice of soldiers sing the song of triumph.'

The chasing of Daphne by Apollo and her dramatic transformation into a bay tree has been a popular subject for art over many centuries – from the Romans to the Renaissance and beyond. Perhaps most famous is a vivid life-sized statue by the Italian sculptor Bernini, in the Galleria Borghese in Rome, which he completed in 1625. It captures the moment where the outstretched hands of the desperate Daphne begin to change to leaves, just as Apollo manages to catch up with her.

Ever afterwards, the Greeks named the bay tree after the heroine of this story – Δάφνη or Dafni – and it was always associated with Apollo. For example, bay leaves formed an important part of the rituals associated with consulting the High Priestess of the Temple of Apollo at Delphi, in ancient Greece. This famous prophet, known as the Pythia or the Oracle of Delphi, was widely sought by persons of status to receive divine inspiration or guidance. Bay was burned in preparation for her prophecy, and during the consultation the Pythia wore a bay leaf crown and carried a branch of the tree, which she shook periodically while in communion with the god Apollo. It is possible that some ancient prophets of this kind even ate bay leaves, and it was also said to inspire dreams of the future if kept by the pillow at night. The Greeks called the bay 'the prophetic plant' and the Roman poet Claudian described it as 'the laurel skilled in what is to happen'.

The Pythian Games were held every four years at Delphi in honour of Apollo, and victorious athletes were given wreaths of bay leaves to wear on their heads. This gradually became extended to other contests and so laurel wreaths became a symbol of victory and status. The Romans adopted this symbolism and their emperors were frequently portrayed wearing a bay wreath, as were victorious generals, as a sign of military success. There was even a custom that dispatches from the front line bringing news of a victory should be wrapped in bay leaves. Even today, bay leaves form an important element of the badge of the Royal Marines, which consists of a world map surrounded by bay leaves – the so-called 'globe and laurel'. European monarchs throughout the centuries have adopted the laurel wreath on their portraits, especially on coins, to demonstrate their power and their military authority – from Napoleon Bonaparte to Tsar Peter the Great to Britain's George III.

Renowned poets were crowned with bay leaves in ancient Greece, since Apollo was the god of poetry. This method of recognising successful poets was continued in the medieval era and Renaissance in parts of Europe such as Italy, and is the origin of the word 'laureate', as in *poet laureate* or *Nobel laureate*. When someone has earned notable success but has then tended to decline, we say they are *resting on their laurels*.

Since ancient times, the bay leaf has been held to have protective powers. Pliny remarks that the bay tree is never struck by lightning, and the Roman Emperor Tiberius

The symbolism of success – the Roman emperor Alexander Severus wears a bay leaf circlet on this coin minted in about AD 230 (left), whilst the 'globe and laurel' badge of the Royal Marines also features bay leaves prominently (right).

reputedly always wore a wreath of bay leaves whenever a storm threatened in order to shield himself from danger. This belief in protection against the power of storms was often described by British authors until the seventeenth century. Greek citizens would hold a leaf in their mouths to provide protection from multiple sources of ill fortune, and the Romans believed that the aroma of the leaves was a defence against infection. It is said that during a contagion in Rome, the Emperor Claudius even transported his whole retinue to Laurentine, a place famous for its masses of bay trees, in order that they might be spared. Their intense odour meant that the leaves were additionally reputed to protect fabric from moths, worms and other types of damage.

At some point the bay tree was brought to the UK and grown here. Medieval English writers were certainly familiar with the bay, but the exact date of introduction is unknown. It is possible that the Romans were responsible. By Tudor times, bay leaves are mentioned as useful to strew across the floor of high status houses to impart a sweet smell to the home. It was widely believed that the bay tree 'withstandeth all evil spirits and enchantments' and this conviction was held even by learned members of society at the time such as doctors. Even in the seventeenth century, the physician and herbalist Nicholas Culpeper confidently asserted the protective powers of bay:

> It is a tree of the Sun, and under the celestial sign Leo, and resisteth witchcraft very potently, as also all the evils old Saturn can do to the body of man, and they are not a few… Neither witch nor devil, thunder nor lightning, will hurt a man in the place where a bay tree is.

A healthy bay tree was thus a potentially valuable protector. However, equally, an ailing plant could be considered a mark of forthcoming human disaster. The Roman historian Suetonius recalled that bay was used as part of the public military celebrations known as 'triumphs' by the rulers of ancient Rome, but the bay trees that each of Caesar's heirs planted on the family estate also announced their deaths. What is more, when Caesar's last direct descendant was assassinated, all the remaining bay trees died to signify the demise of his house:

> The laurel groves flourished so much, that the Caesars procured from them the boughs and crowns they bore at their triumphs. It was also their constant custom to plant others on the same spot, immediately after a triumph; and it was observed that, a little before the death of each prince, the tree which had been set by him died away. But in the last year of Nero, the whole plantation of laurels perished to the very roots.

A similar tale is told in Shakespeare's play *Richard II*, suggesting that the tradition of bay trees foretelling important deaths was still familiar in Elizabethan England. An army captain is sure the monarch has died because of the portents he has observed:

'Tis thought the king is dead; we will not stay.
The bay-trees in our country are all wither'd
And meteors fright the fixed stars of heaven…

Various authors claim magical properties for the bay tree too. For example, the thirteenth-century saint Albertus Magnus related that wrapping a precious opal in a bay leaf could render the bearer invisible. Many sources attest to the ability of bay leaves to influence sleep. The author Richard Brathwaite wrote of bay in 1634: 'if you put his leaves but under your pillow, you shall be sure to have true dreames.' It was an old British custom for young women to lay bay leaves on their pillows on Valentine's Day and they would then dream of their future husbands. An ancient Greek custom was to burn laurel leaves in front of someone you admired and the smell was said to excite their love for you.

Given its reputation for being protective, it is not surprising that the bay tree also had medicinal properties attributed to it. In 1670, John Swan described some of them:

The leaves are hot and dry in the second degree: they resist drunkenness; they gently bind and help diseases in the bladder; help the stinging of bees and wasps; mitigate the pain of the stomach; dry and heal open obstructions of the liver and spleen; resist the pestilence.

Culpeper echoes these uses, and explains some further medicinal uses. He advocates the berries of the bay tree as having special value:

They likewise procure women's courses [menstruations]: and seven of them given to a woman in sore travail of child-birth do cause a speedy delivery, and expel the after-birth, and therefore not to be taken but by such as have gone out their time, lest they procure abortion, or cause labour too soon; they wonderfully help all cold and rheumatic distillations from the brain to the eyes, lungs, or other parts; and being made into an electuary with honey, do help the consumption [TB], old coughs, shortness of breath, and thin rheums; as also the megrim [migraine]; they mightily expel wind, and provoke urine, help the mother, and kill the worms; the leaves also work the like effects.

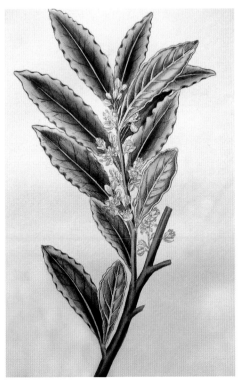

Hand-coloured nineteenth-century print of bay.

A bay tree sapling in a garden pot (top) and bay tree tubs outside business premises (bottom) may hark back to days when these trees were kept nearby to protect against evil.

The Scottish botanist John Claudius Loudon remarked in 1838 that the bay tree was 'very tenacious of life' and even when hacked down to ground level it would often still regenerate. He noted that mature trees could grow to a large size:

> The rate of growth in the neighbourhood of London, as deduced from the dimensions of several young plants sent us, is about 15ft in height in 10 years… The largest tree of this species in England is at Margram in Glamorganshire, the seat of C.P. Talbot, Esq. MP, about 12 miles from Swansea. It is 61ft 6in high, and forms a magnificent bell-shaped bush about 6ft in diameter at the base.

These days, the most familiar use of bay is not to celebrate victory, repel lightning or heal the spleen but as a savoury flavouring agent in cookery. It is generally seen as a desirable component of any 'kitchen garden' and although the tree can eventually reach an enormous size, a small one can be grown in a tub and kept pruned to an attractive shape. Bay's reputed ability to repel infection and the evil eye is often given as a reason for bay trees being habitually planted by the doors of houses: they were guardians against harm reaching the home. However, a ready supply of a handy culinary ingredient within easy picking distance of the kitchen is a more practical explanation.

Beech

Mature beech avenue

*B*eech trees are tall and sturdy, yet elegant, with particularly smooth silver-grey bark. Their beautiful lime green leaves in spring are a vivid contrast to the spring flowers of the forest floor such as bluebells. Although a much admired tree, some beech enthusiasts can perhaps go too far. The Roman orator and consul Passienus Crispus loved one beautiful beech tree so much that he would pour wine on its roots, and even used to embrace it. 'Tree-hugging' is not a modern phenomenon.

There are a number of famous beeches in the UK. Historically, the forest known as Burnham Beeches in Buckinghamshire has long been renowned for the beauty of the woodland and the ancient beeches that live within it. It attracted the attention of writers and artists alike, being within relatively easy travelling distance from London. In 1737, the poet Thomas Gray wrote to a friend describing Burnham: 'Both vale and hill are covered with most venerable beeches and other reverend vegetables.' The trees there have been pollarded as a source of timber for centuries and many of them are hundreds of years old. When one of the largest and most ancient beech specimens at Burnham called 'The Monarch' was toppled in a storm in 1875, it was of such widespread interest that it was reported in *The Times*.

The fresh lime green leaves of young beech trees in spring contrasting exquisitely with bluebells.

Burnham beeches in a sketch from about 1870.

Another celebrated location for venerable beeches can be found in Dorset. The B3082 is a road connecting the towns of Wimborne and Blandford, but rather remarkably it is flanked on either side by a lengthy procession of large beech trees that in the summer create a natural green tunnel 2 miles long. They were planted in the 1830s by William Bankes, a former aide-de-camp of the Duke of Wellington, who owned the Kingston Lacy estate. He planted 365 trees on one side of the road – one for every day of the year – and 366 on the other side for a leap year. The trees still stand, but some have had to be replaced due to disease.

In the neighbouring county of Wiltshire stands a far smaller collection of beech trees – the so-called 'four sisters' of Avebury. These trees stand tightly packed together within the famous stone circle, and their impressive roots bulge out of the firm soil to form a complex intertwining network. Given their mystical location and most unusual appearance, it is no surprise that the sisters have attracted a magical reputation. Many people today make wishes there and tie ribbons to parts of the trees as offerings to the tree spirits.

The diarist and medical practitioner John Evelyn had a particular interest in trees and wrote about the common species encountered in Britain. He explained the extensive use of beech wood for a wide variety of purposes in the seventeenth century:

With it the turner makes dishes, trays, rims for buckets, trenchers [= serving boards], dresser boards, and other utensils. It serves the wheeler and joiner for large

The 'four sisters' of Avebury.

screws etc. The upholsterer uses it for sellies [= wheel rims], chairs, bed-steads etc. It makes shovels and spade-graffs for the husbandman, and is useful to the bellows-maker. It is good for fuel, billet, bavin [= firewood], and coals, though one of the least lasting, and its shavings are good for fining wine. Peter Crescentius writes that the ashes of beech, with proper mixture, is excellent to makes glass with. If the timber lie altogether under water, 'tis little inferior to elm as I find practised and asserted by shipwrights.

The association with shipbuilding is referred to by other writers. Traditionally, for example, it was the wood from which the *Argo* was made – the ship that Jason and the Argonauts took in search of the golden fleece.

However, Evelyn did not write entirely in favour of beech wood. He goes on to say that although it was widely used to make furniture, he deplored the practice because beech was so prone to destruction by woodworm: 'It is so obnoxious that I wish the use of it were, by a law, prohibited all joiners, cabinet-makers, and such as furnish tables, chairs, bed-steads, coffers, screws etc.'

Veteran beech trees lose their youthful
good looks and become gnarled.

Around 150 years later, the botanist James Smith took a similar view of the value of beech as timber. It was not fit, he said, for housebuilding or anything of quality or resilience because when exposed to the alternating dry and wet conditions so common in this country, it tended to decay quickly. He does, however, describe some interesting additional uses:

It is in great demand for cheap furniture, mill-work, screws, and wooden machinery of all kinds, and for the various articles manufactured by the cooper and turner. Its durability under water renders it peculiarly applicable for piles, weirs, sluices, and similar work intended to be constantly wet. The same quality recommends it for the wooden soles of shoes and pattens [clogs], while in France it is preferred to any other wood for making sabots [wooden shoes]… In Germany, thin slices of beech-wood are used by the bookbinders instead of pasteboard for forming sides to thick volumes.

Having been dismissive of the value of the timber, Evelyn was, however, delighted with one particular use made of another part of the beech tree:

But there is yet another benefit which this tree presents us; that its very leaves – which make a natural and most agreeable canopy all the summer – being gathered about the fall [i.e. autumn], and somewhat before they are much frost-bitten, afford the best and easiest mattress in the world to lay under our quilts instead of straw. Because, besides their tenderness and loose lying together, they continue sweet for seven or eight years long, before which straw becomes musty and hard. They are thus used by diverse persons of quality in Dauphine, and in Switzerland. I have sometimes lain on them to my great refreshment.

Beech nuts or 'mast' were valuable products of the tree. The mast was a source of food for fattening pigs and deer, and impoverished people sometimes ate them too. Eating the leaves was believed to be particularly good for the health of teeth and gums. Many authors noted that the beech tree sustains a wide variety of wildlife from birds to squirrels; the Roman writer, Pliny, for example:

The beech is particularly agreeable to rats and mice; and hence it is, that where this tree abounds, those creatures are sure to be plentiful also. The leaves are also very fattening for dormice, and good for thrushes too.

An eighteenth-century depiction of beech, showing its leaves and mast.

Pliny's interest in fattening dormice is probably because the Romans ate them.

Herbalist Nicholas Culpeper described the value of the mast for fattening animals, but he advised that beech had value as a medicine too:

> It is a plant of Saturn, and therefore performs his qualities and proportion in these operations. The leaves of the beech-tree are cooling and binding, and therefore good to be applied to hot swellings to discuss [= dispel] them; the nuts do much nourish such beasts as feed thereon. The water that is found in the hollow places of decaying beeches will cure both man and beast of any scurf, scab, or running tetters [= skin disease], if they be washed therewith; you may boil the leaves into a poultice, or make an ointment of them when time of year serves.

In the reign of Queen Anne, at the beginning of the eighteenth century, a man named Aaron Hill proposed that a whole industry of great value might be created by extracting oil from beech nuts. He even prophesied that the industry would earn enough income to pay off the entire national debt, then estimated at £16 million! He successfully persuaded many people to invest thousands of pounds in his scheme without appreciating the enormous organisation and effort required to yield a quite small amount of oil from a very large number of nuts. Needless to say, it was a get-rich-quick scheme that speedily collapsed and Mr Hill went bust.

One last use – or perhaps *abuse* – of the beech tree must also be mentioned. At least as far back as Roman times the smooth grey bark of the beech has presented a tempting blank canvas to would-be writers. In particular, lovers might be inclined to carve their

Carving lovers' names on a beech tree is an ancient practice.

names upon it. The Roman poet Ovid composed a fictional letter from Oenone to her husband Paris, who had run away with Helen of Troy. In it she reproaches him by reminding him of the romantic times of their youth:

> The beeches still preserve my name carved by your hand; and 'Oenone', the work of your pruning-knife, is read upon their bark; and, as the trunks increase, the letters still dilate.

In *As You Like It*, Shakespeare mentions the custom of lovers carving names on trees, although he does not identify the beech tree specifically: 'There is a man haunts the forest, that abuses our young plants with carving "Rosalind" on their barks.' Many other poets and writers cite this practice. An extreme example once stood at Wittenham Clumps, in Oxfordshire. Here, a man named Joseph Tubb composed a twenty-line poem and carved it into a beech tree in the 1840s. Unfortunately the poem tree died in the 1990s.

Germanic tribes are said to have cut beech tablets to write upon, before the invention of paper, and interestingly the Old Saxon word for writing tablets is *bōk*. Compare this with the Old English for beech, which is *bóece* or *bóc*, and it is easy to see why some scholars believe that our modern word 'book' has its origins in an ancient name for the beech tree.

A beautiful example of the copper beech, the most popular cultivar, and probably first created at the beginning of the nineteenth century as an ornamental variety.

Birch

Silver birch bark and leaf.

*T*his tree's English name is of ancient origin, and as far back as the eighth century, the Anglo-Saxons were writing about the *berc* or *birce*. There are actually two native species in the UK: the silver (or white) birch, named of course because of its eye-catching bark, and the downy birch, which has a very similar appearance. Birches are rather elegant or dainty trees and thus were formerly referred to as 'lady birch'.

The birch is fast-growing and produces a great quantity of seed, so it is quick to colonise new areas of open land, even in colder European countries where it seems most at home. Pollen analysis shows it was one of the first trees to colonise Britain after the last ice age.

Perhaps the first significant appearance of birch in the history of the UK was as the medium on which the Vindolanda tablets were created. These thin slices of wood were written upon in ink by Roman officers stationed at Hadrian's Wall, and birch was probably chosen because it grew abundantly in the vicinity. The tablets were thin – up to 3mm thickness – and about the size of a postcard. Birch was a common wood used, but alder and oak are also seen. The tablets have been called Britain's most important archaeological treasure and they provide a fascinating first-hand account of everyday life at a Roman frontier in the first century.

Ironically, given that the birch is so common, its timber has generally been avoided in England and Wales for prestigious or higher profile functions such as the manufacture of furniture, woodcarving, or for constructing buildings. Even in the seventeenth century, John Evelyn described it as 'of all other, the worst of timber'. Birch wood made cheap

Birch saplings can quickly colonise a new area of open ground.

pit props and sleepers for rural cart trails, short-lasting yokes for oxen, and it could be cut to make rough and ready domestic items such as serving boards and bowls, but as far as many of our ancestors were concerned its most popular use was simply as firewood.

Having said this, birch wood was much more appreciated in areas such as the north of Scotland, where there were limited alternative local sources of timber. Walter Nicol and Edward Sang described the contemporary use of birch wood in Scotland in *The Planter's Kalendar*, published in 1812:

> Birch may be said to be the universal wood of the Scots Highlanders. They make everything of it: they build their houses of it; make their beds, chairs, tables, dishes, and spoons of it; construct their mills of it; make their carts, ploughs, harrows, gates, and fences of it; and even manufacture ropes of it!

Two decades or so later, John Loudon further reported upon the use of birch trees in Scotland and provided more detail about the Highlanders' methods:

> The branches are employed as fuel in the distillation of whisky; and they are found to contribute a flavour to it far superior to that produced by the use of fir-wood, coal, or peat. Birch spray [= twigs] is also used for smoking hams and herrings, for which last purpose it is preferred to every other kind of wood. The bark is used for tanning leather, dyeing yellow, making ropes, and sometimes, as in Lapland, instead of candles. The spray is used for thatching houses; and, dried in summer with the leaves on, it makes an excellent material for sleeping upon where heath is scarce. The wood was formerly used in the Highlands for arrows.

One common way to make use of birch was to cut off some of the slender twigs and tie them to a long handle to make a broom or besom for sweeping away rubbish. As long ago as the thirteenth century this usage was referred to: 'therewith houses being swept and cleansed'. They looked like witches' broomsticks. Similar bunches of birch twigs were commonly utilised as part of the 'beating the bounds' ceremony that many parishes invoked to ensure that their boundaries and jurisdictions were properly known and enforced each year. This event was often initiated by the Church, and it was young boys who typically carried the birch twigs with which they beat the parish boundary markers, thus ensuring that future generations would recall the legal limits of parish authority. Sometimes the boys themselves were beaten to help them remember this important local knowledge!

Bound birch twigs or a birch rod were an allowable means for thrashing certain offenders as well. Indeed, the old phrase 'to send someone to Birching Lane' meant to arrange for them to be punished. Medieval illuminated manuscripts show boys in particular being beaten with 'the birch', and William Turner in his herbal states that the birch 'serveth for beating of stubborn boys'. But girls were not exempt.

Children at school were commonly beaten with the birch up until the mid-1800s, and some public schools such as Eton became notorious for their zeal in administering it. According to a description of the school's punishment tool in the 1870s: 'The usual rod at Eton consisted of three long birchen twigs (no branches), bound with a string for about a quarter of their length.' A list of victims was drawn up each week, and the flogging was delivered to each boy's bared buttocks every Friday. Dr John Keate was in charge of Eton from 1809 to 1834, and earned a reputation as the school's greatest flogging headmaster. His punishments were frequent and he was determined that none should ever escape what he deemed to be due; this led to many anecdotes about his behaviour from former pupils such as this one:

An illustration of a boy being birched from James Le Palmer's fourteenth-century encyclopedia *Omne Bonum*, compiled in London. (*Courtesy of the British Library illuminated manuscripts collection www.bl.uk*)

Among the many good stories told of 'Old Keate', perhaps the best is that of the boy who called on him to take leave.

'You seem to know me very well,' said the great headmaster, 'but I have no remembrance of ever having seen your face before.'

'You were better acquainted, sir, with my other end,' was the unblushing reply.

The use of the birch was commonly invoked by the law and its officers as well. As recently as 1879, the Summary Jurisdiction Act maintained that if a child was charged with any indictable offence other than murder, then either in addition to or instead of any other punishment, a boy could be 'privately whipped with not more than six strokes of a birch rod by a constable'. A youth could be given up to twelve strokes.

A less brutal use for bundles of birch twigs in recent times has been the gentle self-flagellation with them that forms part of taking a sauna in Finland. For this reason and many others, the birch itself is much appreciated in Finland and is officially that country's national tree.

Apart from harvesting the twigs and branches of birch, the sap was extracted from living trees by a process of tapping. John Pechey, the seventeenth-century herbalist, says the birch 'yields plentifully a sweet and potulent juice, which shepherds, when they are thirsty, often drink in the woods'. The sap was used to make what was called 'birch wine' and this was manufactured on a large scale. The liquid was drawn off by boring

A mature silver birch tree; the slender branches can get longer with age and give the tree a 'weeping' effect.

holes in the trunks in around March, when the sap was rising but before the leaves appeared. Quills were inserted into the holes so that the juice drained out into buckets or bottles placed under the trees. Large trees were tapped in several places and by this method, considerable volumes of sap could be collected in just a few days. The estate of the naturalist Sir Joseph Banks in Ashover, Derbyshire, held a grove of about one hundred birch trees that by 1813 had been harvested continuously for seventy years to provide birch juice. Some trees would yield as much as two gallons of juice in a day, but the average was about a pint. One tree could produce as much as thirty or forty gallons of juice in a season.

To make the wine, birch juice was boiled, skimming off the scum in the process, before cooling and fermenting it with the aid of yeast. Sometimes sugar, honey, raisins or cloves were added. When properly manufactured it was said to be a most cooling and agreeable

Early nineteenth-century illustration of the silver birch and its catkins.

drink. Both the raw juice and birch wine was described in the seventeenth century as 'a great opener, and reputed to be a powerful curer of the tissick'; in other words, it was a laxative and valued as a treatment for chest diseases such as tuberculosis. Its other medicinal powers included treating kidney stones, scurvy, sore mouths, jaundice, and warts. Rather oddly, birch juice was also claimed to preserve cheese from being eaten by worms.

Cherry

Freshly picked cherries.

Perhaps the most famous story about a cherry tree is the tale of George Washington, who as a six-year-old boy was, rather curiously, given a hatchet as a present. He apparently went around his father's garden chopping things and then, according to his unreliable biographer Parson Weems, 'he unluckily tried the edge of his hatchet on the body of a beautiful young English cherry-tree, which he barked so terribly, that I don't believe the tree ever got the better of it.' The next morning his father noticed the damage and called his son to him:

George Washington and the cherry tree.

> 'George,' said his father, 'do you know who killed that beautiful little cherry tree yonder in the garden?'
>
> This was a tough question; and George staggered under it for a moment; but quickly recovered himself: and looking at his father, with the sweet face of youth brightened with the inexpressible charm of all-conquering truth, he bravely cried out, 'I can't tell a lie, Pa; you know I can't tell a lie. I did cut it with my hatchet.'
>
> 'Run to my arms, you dearest boy,' cried his father in transports, 'run to my arms; glad am I, George, that you killed my tree; for you have paid me for it a thousand fold. Such an act of heroism in my son is more worth than a thousand trees, though blossomed with silver, and their fruits of purest gold.'

This tale was promoted to illustrate the importance of telling the truth even if it meant taking the blame for something, and in so doing it extolled the virtues of the saintly George Washington who was widely idolised. It is a sentimentalised account intended to appeal to a Christian society, and is told in the sickly sweet, moralising language of the early nineteenth century. Many believe that this was a fable invented by Weems in order to sell his book about Washington, but it is now probably impossible to know for certain whether there was ever any truth in it.

The cherry tree has occasional Christian connections in English folklore. For example, a legend tells how the Virgin Mary longed to taste some tempting cherries hanging on a tree above her head. She could not reach them herself, so she asked her husband Joseph to pick them. Joseph, apparently still upset after discovering that God had made his wife pregnant, refused to gather the cherries, saying sullenly, 'Let the father of your child present you with the cherries.' No sooner had he said this, than the branch of the cherry tree bent itself down for Mary, and she plucked the fruit and ate it. There was also a myth that Jesus once gave a cherry to St Peter, apparently as some sort of reproof, cautioning him not to despise small things.

In the UK, cherries have long been sold on the streets. Everyone enjoyed cherries, hence the old phrase: 'A cherry year, a merry year; a plum year, a dumb year.' Although grown all over England, Kent was the traditional home of this industry: miles of orchards grew there even in Edwardian times. The beginning of the cherry season was often marked by the parading of a bough through the centre of London, loaded with fruits. The cry of the street sellers is believed to have inspired lines by English composer Thomas Campion, probably written in the sixteenth century: 'There cheries grow, that none may buy; Till cherie ripe ripe ripe themselves do crie.' The opening lines to Robert Herrick's romantic poem *Cherry Ripe*, written in the seventeenth century, are similar:

The street seller of cherries. (*Courtesy of Wellcome Collection https://wellcomecollection.org*)

> *Cherry-ripe, ripe, ripe, I cry,*
> *Full and fair ones; come, and buy.*
> *If so be you ask me where*
> *They do grow? I answer, there*
> *Where my Julia's lips do smile.*
> *There's the land, or cherry-isle,*
> *Whose plantations fully show*
> *All the year where cherries grow.*

Herrick's poem later gave rise to a popular song called *Cherry Ripe* with music by Charles Horn, which was based on the poem, using the first two lines as a refrain. This song was immensely popular and is often cited in literature of the late nineteenth and early twentieth centuries. It is mentioned in George Eliot's *Middlemarch* (1881) for example, John Buchan's *Mr Standfast* (1918), and Dylan Thomas's *A Child's Christmas in Wales* (1952).

Lofty wild cherry trees in flower; unlike most commercial and garden varieties, they can grow to 90 feet high or more.

There are two species of cherry that are native to the UK: the bird cherry and the wild cherry. These native cherry trees are much hardier and larger than the modern varieties grown to produce the fruit that we eat today. The fruit of native trees are much smaller, too, and fairly sparse in number, hence the old proverb: 'One cherry tree sufficeth not two jays.' In other words, the crop from an average tree was only likely to sustain a single bird. Native cherries can be rather sharp tasting or bitter and, since these trees are often quite tall, the birds usually reach them before people can get anywhere near.

In former centuries, native cherries were called 'geans' in the UK, and some darker varieties from the West Country were termed 'mazzards'. Different varieties of cultivated cherry have been known since at least Roman times. The historian Pliny, writing in the first century AD, states that nine different varieties of cherry were known in his time:

Of this fruit, that known as the 'Apronian' is the reddest variety, the 'Lutatian' being the blackest, and the 'Cæcilian' perfectly round. The 'Junian' cherry has an agreeable flavour, but only, so to say, when eaten beneath the tree, as they are so remarkably delicate that they will not bear carrying. The highest rank, however, has been awarded to the 'Duracinus' variety, known in Campania as the 'Plinian' cherry, and in Belgica as the 'Lusitanian' cherry, as also to one that grows on the banks of the Rhenus. This last kind has a third colour, being a mixture of black, red, and green, and has always the appearance of being just on the turn to ripening. It is less than five years since the kind known as the 'laurel-cherry' was introduced, of a bitter but not unpleasant flavour, the produce of a graft upon the laurel. The 'Macedonian' cherry grows on a tree that is very small, and rarely exceeds three cubits in height; while the 'Chamaecerasus' is still smaller, being but a mere shrub.

The distinctive bark with horizontal lenticles that marks the wild cherry tree.

A Roman myth held that cherries were first brought to Italy from the east by the general and politician Lucullus, after his military campaigns of the first century BC. This is incorrect because cherry stones have been found in Roman archaeological digs that predate Lucullus, but he probably returned to Rome with a particularly admired variety. Nevertheless, Pliny states that the spread of cherry trees throughout

Cherries almost ready for picking.

Europe was all thanks to Lucullus: 'in the course of one hundred and twenty years after him, other lands had cherries – even beyond the ocean as far as Britain.' The Roman name for the cherry was *cerasus*, which was the name of the town in Anatolia (modern Turkey) from which Lucullus is said to have brought his cherries.

Although Pliny was aware of nine varieties, by the 1820s there were around 250 varieties known to growers in England. The easy availability of cherries in season led to their being widely eaten. Cherry juice was popular as a flavouring, and to produce alcoholic drinks such as cherry brandy or 'cherry bounce'. The latter was popular and sparked a humorous song that satirised Robert Herrick's poem *Cherry ripe*:

> *Cherry bounce, cherry bounce, bounce, I cry,*
> *Fill a glass on the sly;*
> *If so be you ask me where,*
> *To the wine-vaults we'll repair;*
> *When we heavy wet renounce,*
> *That's the time for cherry bounce!*

A number of other alcoholic cherry beverages have been produced around Europe including maraschino from Italy, kirsch from Germany, and various types of cherry vodka such as wiśniówka from Poland.

In societies with limited forms of leisure activity, cherries are even known to have formed the basis of at least two games. In medieval times the game of 'bob cherry' involved trying to grab a cherry on a string with your teeth. In the sixteenth and seventeenth centuries, 'cherry pit' was a game played by throwing cherry stones into a small hole.

Cherries were commonplace and the old saying 'It's not worth a cherry stone' indicated that something was worthless. A more familiar phrase that is still used is 'to take two bites of the cherry'. These days it implies that someone has managed to have a second attempt at something. However, the original phrase meant something quite different. Cherries were so small that none but the daintiest of eaters would do anything but eat them at one bite. Those who took two bites of the cherry were therefore people who behaved with affected manners. The Italian writer Torriano described the phrase nicely in 1662: 'To play the hypocrite, and be demure, are [they] that will make two bites of one cherry, but in private can devour a pound and more.' It seems to have evolved into a way of describing someone who will sub-divide even a small task, before acquiring its modern meaning.

These days, cultivated trees that produce cherries are usually classified as sweet cherries that can be eaten raw, or sour cherries that need to be processed in some way before eating. Sour cherries are often baked for pies, cooked to make

Medieval illustration of the game of bob cherry from the *Queen Mary Psalter*, dating to 1310–20. (*Courtesy of the British Library illuminated manuscripts collection www. bl.uk*)

conserves, or utilised in the manufacture of various kinds of drink. Apart from their use as food, cherries were sometimes claimed to have medicinal properties, particularly for treating kidney and bladder complaints. Writing in 1694, herbalist John Pechey described some of the other properties attributed to them:

> Cherries, when they are fresh, loosen the belly; but when dry, they bind. Those that are sweet, purge; but they are offensive to the stomach. Sharp and harsh cherries are binding. The distill'd water of sharp cherries, and the cherries themselves extinguish feverish heats, and quench thirst, and create an appetite. And, preserv'd with sugar, they are very grateful to the stomach, and reckon'd by the women the best sweet-meats; but, by reason of the abundance of their moisture, they cannot be kept long.
>
> The decoction of dried cherries is excellent in hypochondriac diseases, and many have been cur'd by this remedy alone. Sweet cherries are peculiarly good for diseases in the head, the falling-sickness [= epilepsy], apoplexy and palsie [= strokes]. A Lord that was seiz'd with an apoplexy, and was speechless three days, recover'd his speech by taking spirit of cherries. In stammering, and other vices of speech, wash the mouth often with the spirit of black cherries for they are very cephalic [= benefit the head], and do much strengthen the muscles of the tongue and the spirits design'd for their use. The distill'd water of sweet black cherries is much commended, and us'd for children's convulsions.

The white blossom of the sweet cherry cultivar 'Nabella'.

Pink flowers of a cultivated Japanese cherry tree.

The wood of the cherry tree has also been popular with wood turners and cabinetmakers because it is hard, has a rich, attractive colour and polishes beautifully. However, almost as well known as the fruit is the beautiful blossom of the cherry tree, which has excited praise for centuries. Indeed, many varieties of cherry have been cultivated solely to produce flowers and they no longer yield fruit.

Nowhere else in the world is cherry blossom more revered than in Japan, where it has been venerated for over a thousand years. The blossom, or *sakura*, is one of the national flowers of Japan along with the chrysanthemum, and news broadcasts every year track the flowering of the trees across the nation. Japanese people enjoy eating a meal and socialising under the *sakura*, and this practice is called *hanami*. The blooms are sometimes eaten or used to make tea. It is hard to explain the deep veneration for cherry blossom in Japan, but it has been said that the brief flowering of the cherry tree is an allegory that appeals to the Japanese consciousness as a metaphor for the transience of beauty, or even of life itself.

A tree inside a tree

The botanist John Lindley described a very unusual cherry tree in 1855:

> In the park of the Duke of Devonshire, at Chiswick, there is a very old cherry tree, which has been decayed in the centre for many years. Its hollow trunk has been occupied by a common birch tree, so that the same stem appears to support a top composed of birch and cherry branches. The cherry trunk is 7½ feet in circumference, and 6 feet in height to the place where the branches diverge from it... [The birch] is now above 50 feet high, and measures 5 feet and 4 inches in circumference at 6 feet from the ground, where it issues from the hollow cherry. The portion of the cherry tree still alive is 20 to 25 feet high.

Elm

Elm leaves.

*I*t's difficult to appreciate just how drastically the UK landscape has changed as a result of Dutch elm disease. The English elm (*Ulmus procera*) was once one of the nation's commonest broadleaved trees, but this infection killed over 60 million of them in two epidemics: one began in the 1920s and the other in the late 1960s. The disease itself is a fungus that is spread by bark beetles. It kills other species of elm as well such as the native wych elm, and non-natives such as the smooth leaved elm and Huntingdon elm, but the English elm was particularly vulnerable. There are still millions of young elms left because the beetle prefers to inhabit the thicker bark of older trees, but almost all the mature specimens have succumbed to the disease.

The largest concentration of remaining old elms can be found in the vicinity of Brighton. Here, the local authority came up with a very successful strategy for combating the disease, helped enthusiastically by a community determined to preserve its elms. Trenches were dug around trees growing close together to prevent the spread of infection via root contact; traps were set for the beetles; and at the first sign of disease, the affected branches were lopped off. Today, there are over 17,000 elms in Brighton and Hove and they have been awarded the status of the UK's National Elm Collection. A pair of these trees, known as the Preston Twins, are around 400 years of age and considered to be the oldest elm trees in the world. Unfortunately, one of the twins was very badly damaged by high winds in August 2017 and may not survive much longer.

There are other large elms dotted around the country. Perhaps surprisingly, there is a notable example in inner London. A large Huntingdon elm stands at the top of Marylebone High Street, having withstood inner-city development, the 'Blitz' bombings of the Second World War, and Dutch elm disease. A true survivor, it is believed to be around 150 years old and towers over neighbouring four-storey buildings.

Yet in the UK, and in the English south and midlands particularly, almost every neighbourhood once had its own famous old elm. Celebrated for their age and size, these venerable titans were often carefully preserved against all the odds, even after becoming badly damaged. Local residents would shore them up with props, bricks, metal bands and concrete to try to keep them going. Many were linked with a historical character and they often had names. Hunter's Elm in Brentwood, Essex was said to have been planted in the 1550s to commemorate a local teenage Protestant martyr burned at the stake by Mary I. Latimer's Elm in Hadley, Hertfordshire was allegedly the tree under which another famous Protestant victim of the same queen, Hugh Latimer, once gave a sermon to Henry VIII. The Queen's Elm formerly stood in Chelsea until it was chopped down in 1745; it was claimed that Elizabeth I herself had actually planted it. In Stony Stratford, Buckinghamshire there formerly stood Wesley's Elm, underneath which John Wesley the Methodist is said to have preached in the open air. And there are many more examples.

The poet Lord Byron was apparently fond of the elm. One elm in particular took his fancy: in 1822 he recalled his favourite spot had been under a large tree in St Mary's churchyard, Harrow, where he 'used to sit for hours and hours when a boy'. This elm became known as Byron's Elm and he even wrote a poem about it in 1807. His *Lines Written Beneath an Elm* contains these words:

A true survivor: the large Huntingdon elm at the top of Marylebone High Street, in London.

Much damaged by a lightning strike, the remains of Byron's Elm in the churchyard at Harrow in about 1910.

> *Thou drooping elm!*
> *Beneath whose boughs I lay,*
> *And frequent mus'd the twilight hours away*

Communities became very attached to their local elm trees. When the Great Exhibition was being planned by the Victorians, it was decided to build what became known as the Crystal Palace in Hyde Park. This purpose-built structure was enormous – covering about 18 acres – and was designed to house a grand international celebration of manufactured products. The exhibition was organised by Henry Cole and Prince Albert, but when the design for the palace became known there was outrage: in order to build the palace, three precious elm trees in Hyde Park would need to be felled. The complaints that followed were so intense that the designer, Joseph Paxton, was obliged to change his plans. The palace would be built, but the living elm trees would be accommodated within it.

Queen Victoria was concerned that the elms attracted sparrows that flew in through the open windows and roosted in the trees, and these might result in visitors being

Mature living elm trees in Hyde Park were accommodated inside the Crystal Palace, built for the Great Exhibition of 1851.

soiled by bird droppings. She is said to have asked the Duke of Wellington for advice and he allegedly replied tersely: 'Sparrowhawks, Ma'am.' And this is apparently what they did – they kept a sparrowhawk in residence to chase away or eat the sparrows.

However, despite being much loved, elm trees also had some sinister historical associations. 'The Elms' in London was a place once synonymous with public execution and originally located outside the city, where elm trees were common and could be used for hangings. Two such places were frequently documented – one in Smithfield and one in Tyburn. One of the earliest references to such an event comes in 1196 when populist leader William FitzOsbert was condemned to death for sedition; a contemporary account says that he was dragged by the heels 'through the centre of the city to the elms, his flesh was demolished and spread all over the pavement and, fettered with a chain, he was hanged that same day on the elms with his associates and died'. Other famous early executions at the elms included the Scottish leader William Wallace, who in 1305 was taken 'through the middle of the city as far as Elms, and for the robberies, murders and felonies which he carried out in the kingdom of England and the land of Scotland he should be hanged there and afterwards drawn'.

The Smithfield site was no longer in operation after the early 1400s, whereas Tyburn was utilised until the eighteenth century. It was located in the modern Marble Arch area of London. Here, people were executed by hanging from the 'Tyburn Tree' – originally a large elm, later a man-made gallows, but the term 'Tyburn Tree' was used for both. They became great public spectacles attended by thousands and were often the place of death for traitors, heretics and murderers. The last execution at Tyburn was the highwayman John Austin, in 1783.

In the past, the elm was so ubiquitous in town and countryside that in London alone there are still over 150 elm-related street names. The tree was sufficiently popular that those with land available might elect to plant themselves an elm

The classic shape and appearance of a mature English elm tree.

woodland, and this was a common enough practice for a specific word to be coined in the English language to describe it – an ulmarium.

Large elm trees have a characteristic shape, often seen in old paintings of the British countryside, but they tend to be fairly shallow rooted and to generate very weighty side branches that cannot be supported by the main trunk, which often becomes hollow with age. This gives mature trees a certain amount of instability. Veteran trees were notoriously prone to suddenly dropping large branches or even falling over completely without warning. This propensity for unpredictability is captured rather delightfully by the children's author Richard Jefferies in his *Wood Magic*, published in 1881:

'You think because the elm has no legs and cannot run after you, and because he has no hands and cannot catch you, that therefore he cannot do you any harm. You are very much mistaken; that is a very malicious elm, and of a very wicked disposition. Elms, indeed, are very treacherous, and I recommend you to have nothing to do with them, dear.'

'But how could he hurt me?' said Bevis.

'He can wait till you go under him,' said the squirrel, 'and then drop that big bough on you. He has had that bough waiting to drop on somebody for quite ten years. Just look up and see how thick it is, and heavy; why, it would smash a man out flat. Now, the reason the elms are so dangerous is because they will wait so long till somebody passes. Trees can do a great deal, I can tell you; why, I have known a tree, when it could not drop a bough, fall down altogether when there was not a breath of wind, nor any lightning, just to kill a cow or a sheep, out of sheer bad temper.'

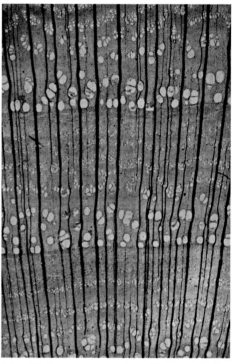

Magnified transverse section of the wood of English elm.

Elm wood was a commercially important material, with a wide variety of roles depending upon its quality, which could vary quite considerably according to its growing conditions. Good quality timber was used for household furniture such as dressers and tables, but most notably perhaps it was a favourite wood for coffins. Even the most privileged might find themselves so interred at the end of their days: after Anne Boleyn's beheading, it was found that officials had forgotten to prepare a coffin, so she was hastily buried in an elm box intended for storing arrows. The nineteenth-century poet Thomas Hood wrote verses entitled *The Elm Tree*, in which he jests that providing coffins is the elm's revenge on humankind for people who chopped them down:

> *This massy trunk that lies along,*
> *And many more must fall –*
> *For the very knave who digs the grave,*
> *The man who spreads the pall,*
> *And he who tolls the funeral bell –*
> *The elm shall have them all!*

Elm wood was widely sought after throughout the building industry for floorboards, roof timbers, fences, gates, weatherboards and so forth. Like oak, it was a tough wood and was selected in situations where strength was important such as wheels, mill workings, chopping blocks, trunks, shields, and even door hinges. It was recognised as being durable in wet conditions where it could survive for decades without rotting, yet unlike alder, which has similar properties, the size of the elm tree enabled its timber to be employed for much bigger projects. This meant it was suitable for large water pipes, lock gates, boat keels, buckets, and piles to support bridges and quays. Old London Bridge was supported by elm trunks for six centuries.

The leaves of elm were sometimes useful to farmers. If dried properly they provided a suitable alternative to hay. The seventeenth-century writer John Evelyn records that dried elm leaves 'will prove a great relief to cattle in winter and scorching summers, when hay and fodder is dear; they will eat them before oats and thrive exceedingly well with them'.

In terms of medicinal value, elm offered a number of traditional properties and John Gerard recorded some of them from the late Tudor period:

> The leaves of elm glue and heal up green wounds, so doth the bark wrapped and swaddled about the wound like a band. The leaves being stamped with vinegar do take away scurffe [a skin condition]… The decoction of elm leaves, as also of bark or root, healeth broken bones very speedily if they be fomented or bathed therewith.

Nicholas Culpeper, writing a little over fifty years later, adds that vinegar-soaked leaves were a valuable treatment for leprosy, and he describes these additional medicinal qualities:

Elms were once common in central London: elms in Knightsbridge in the 1890s.

Some of the twenty-eight elm saplings planted in George Street, Marylebone, London in about 2010. One tree was planted in nearby Bolsover Street, since Byron used to live there.

The roots of the elm, boiled for a long time in water, and the fat arising on the top thereof being clean scummed off, and the place anointed therewith that is grown bald, and the hair fallen away, will quickly restore them again. The said bark ground with brine and pickle, until it come to the form of a poultice, and laid on the place pained with the gout, giveth great ease. The decoction of the bark in water, is excellent to bathe such places as have been burnt with fire.

A revival for the elm is long overdue. Unfortunately, all of the naturally occurring elm species are susceptible to Dutch elm disease, although some are less prone than others. Research to create disease-resistant cultivars continues. Nonetheless, elms are still planted and some do survive. In 2009, for example, the London inner-city area of Marylebone began a programme of tree planting that included numerous elms. One day, perhaps, the elm will flourish again; a tree that 'has a right, both with respect to beauty and utility, to claim a place next to the oak in dignity and rank'.

Woolf amongst the elms

The pioneering writer Virginia Woolf lived in London for much of her life, where elm trees were abundant at the beginning of the twentieth century. In her novel *Mrs Dalloway*, published in 1925, she captures the beauty of a London elm tree in full leaf:

> The excitement of the elm trees rising and falling, rising and falling with all their leaves alight and the colour thinning and thickening from blue to the green of a hollow wave, like plumes on horses' heads, feathers on ladies', so proudly they rose and fell, so superbly.

When she moved to Sussex, she was delighted by two intertwined elms in her back garden, which she called Virginia and Leonard, after herself and her husband. Sadly, in 1941 Virginia Woolf committed suicide, but her body was cremated and the ashes buried beneath her beloved elms.

Hawthorn

The blossom of common hawthorn attracts many insects.

*T*he common hawthorn (*Crataegus monogyna*) is perhaps the most mystical of all trees found in the UK, and there are many superstitions and traditions associated with it. Hawthorns are hardy plants that will grow in quite demanding conditions, and so it is not uncommon to find a lone tree growing in an unlikely and remote place: on a wind-blasted hill, sprouting from a clifftop, and so on. Our ancestors seem to have taken this tenacious survival as a sign of some sort of magical protection, especially in Ireland, which may explain its frequent association with fairies, elves and similar sprites. For example, in a once popular thirteenth-century myth, the Scottish laird Thomas the Rhymer met the Queen of Elfland by a hawthorn tree and was then conducted to her realm. In Arthurian legend, one version of the death of Merlin the wizard describes how he was trapped forever in an enchanted hawthorn by the fairy Viviane, known as the Lady of the Lake. In Ireland, a kind of mischievous fairy called the phooka is said to have taken pity on a group of Irish rebels trapped by a large army. The chieftain of the besieging army was enticed to a nearby hawthorn tree where he was trapped with spider's silk, leaving the phooka to adopt his likeness and simply lead the besieging army away so that the rebels could escape. In some parts of the UK, the hawthorn was even known as the fairy tree.

It was held to be especially important not to cut flowers or branches from a hawthorn that was favoured by fairies or elves without permission, as it would provoke resentment and therefore bad luck. These lone sentinel hawthorns were often quite elderly, and a community could become obsessive about the dangers of damaging them. An example is highlighted in a report from the vicinity of Newparish in Scotland, in 1796:

> There is a quick thorn of a very antique appearance, for which the people have a superstitious veneration. They have a mortal dread to lop off or cut any part of it, and affirm with a religious horror, that some persons who had the temerity to hurt it were afterwards severely punished for their sacrilege.

Community protection, or even veneration, means that some hawthorns have survived hundreds of years. In the village of Hethel in Norfolk there grows a tree known as the Old Thorn, which was possibly planted in the thirteenth century and so is now over 700 years old. It may be the oldest hawthorn in England, but if not it is certainly one of the oldest. Its importance is such that it has become its own small nature reserve at around 0.025 hectares. In 1755, its girth was measured at just over 9 feet but although still living, its bulk has considerably decreased with age since then.

You don't have to look very far afield to find alleged cases of landowners and farmers who went against the practice of protecting a community's special hawthorn and who subsequently suffered dire consequences. However, since it was not possible to be sure which individual hawthorns were supernaturally favoured, a widespread custom was to say 'thank you' or to make an apology out loud every time a branch was cut, just in case. It was often considered unlucky to cut branches and bring them indoors – this act could bring misfortune upon the person who did it – but if fixed to the outside of the house

Isolated hawthorn trees fascinated and awed our ancestors because of the mystical powers believed to be associated with them.

the hawthorn was believed to protect the home from invasion by evil spirits or from being struck by lightning.

Another mystical story involving the hawthorn provides a further link to Arthurian folklore. Joseph of Arimathea is cited in the New Testament as a wealthy man who asked for the body of Christ after his crucifixion, in order to inter him in a tomb. Legend has it that Joseph was later entrusted with the Holy Grail, which he brought to England. On arrival, a local chieftain allowed him to live in the area around Glastonbury, known as Avalon, where he stuck his walking stick into the ground and it grew into a hawthorn that blossomed on Christmas day. This 'Glastonbury thorn' is a distinct variety of hawthorn that flowers twice a year. It has been symbolically important to the Church because this flowering occurs around about the time of the two most

Early fourteenth-century depiction of Joseph of Arimathea preaching to his followers. (*Courtesy of the British Library illuminated manuscripts collection www.bl.uk*)

important Christian festivals of Easter and Christmas. Christians held for many centuries that the hawthorn had actually been used to create Christ's crown of thorns that he wore while being crucified. Some even said that Joseph of Arimathea's staff that grew into the Glastonbury Thorn had been cut from the self-same tree.

The oldest surviving Glastonbury thorn tree was cut down by a Puritan soldier during the English Civil War as it was considered an inappropriate object of veneration. Inevitably, the thorns of the falling tree were said to have caught his face and blinded him as punishment.

However, cuttings from the most elderly Glastonbury thorns have been repeatedly taken over the centuries to ensure that legacy trees survive. In the seventeenth century, a custom arose during the reign of James I of sending a spray of Glastonbury thorn blossom to the sovereign on Christmas Day.

Royal badge of Henry VII showing his crown lodged in a hawthorn. (*Courtesy of the British Library illuminated manuscripts collection www.bl.uk*)

This practice continues, and a twig bearing flowers is delivered to the monarch in time for 25 December every year by the Mayor of Glastonbury and the Vicar of St John The Baptist's Church, where the hawthorns grow.

There are other royal connections with hawthorn. There is a story that after the Battle of Bosworth Field in 1485, the crown of the defeated Richard III was found by Henry VII's supporters in a hawthorn tree. This explains why Henry later adopted a crowned hawthorn with the letters 'HR' as one of his royal badges. There was even an Old English proverb that arose as a consequence: 'Cleave to the crown, though it hang on a bush' – in other words, be loyal to the sovereign no matter how they came by their authority. Mary Queen of Scots is another monarch associated with the hawthorn, and she is reputed to have personally planted a number of them. A venerable specimen known as 'Queen Mary's Thorn' at Duddingston, Edinburgh survived 300 years until it was blown down by a gale in 1836.

The month of May was when the hawthorn was said to produce the greatest abundance of its white flowers, hence they were usually called 'may blossom' and the hawthorn was commonly known as the may tree or whitethorn. The flowers appear in abundance and are very attractive, capturing the attention of poets down the ages. In *Henry VI (part 3)*, Shakespeare wrote:

The smell of death?

In the nineteenth century it was recorded that some rural communities perpetuated a belief that the aroma of hawthorn flowers resembled the smell of the Great Plague of 1665. Interestingly, one of the chemicals responsible for the flowers' scent is trimethylamine, which is also found in decaying tissue. This odour may be used by the plant to attract flies that feed on carrion to act as pollinators. There are in fact two species of hawthorn in the UK. The Midland hawthorn or 'woodland hawthorn' (*Crataegus laevigata*) is less frequently seen than the common hawthorn, but it may have been more widespread in the past and it has a much stronger smell.

A pink variety of the Midland hawthorn (*Crataegus laevigata*).

> Gives not the hawthorn-bush a sweeter shade
> To shepherds looking on their silly sheep,
> Than doth a rich embroider'd canopy
> To kings that fear their subjects' treachery?

In former times, the first day of May marked a nationwide day of local festivities in the UK to commemorate the beginning of summer, and May Day celebrations involved cutting branches of may blossom and displaying them above doorways. Significantly, hawthorn flowers were used to decorate the top of the Maypole, around which a community would dance. The origins of May Day itself probably lie in pagan ceremonies such as the Roman festivities to honour the goddess of flowers, Flora, and the ancient Gaelic custom known as Beltane. The special circumstance of May Day also offered a chance for women to use the hawthorn to preserve their beauty into old age:

Maypole with village children dancing to celebrate May Day in about 1910.

> *The fair maid who, the first of May,*
> *Goes to the fields at break of day,*
> *And washes in dew from the hawthorn tree,*
> *Will ever after handsome be.*

The fact that the month of May and hawthorn blossom have the same name has led to some uncertainty about the precise meaning of some old sayings. A famous one is: 'Ne'er cast a clout till may be out.' The word 'clout' refers to clothing, and the phrase means that you shouldn't take off your warm winter clothes until may is out – but does that mean when the may blossom appears or when the month of May is finished? People disagree on this. Personally, I think the reference is to hawthorn blossom simply because keeping winter clothes on until 31 May seems far too pessimistic, even for a nation that constantly complains about its bad weather.

Another well-known example of ambiguous use of the word 'may' is found in Shakespeare's sonnet number 18:

> *Shall I compare thee to a Summer's day?*
> *Thou art more lovely and more temperate.*
> *Rough winds do shake the darling buds of May,*
> *And Summer's lease hath all too short a date.*

To my mind, this is an even more explicit reference to hawthorn, rather than the month, but I doubt we will ever know for certain. A key phrase from this Shakespearian sonnet – *The Darling Buds of May* – was the title of a novel about the Larkin family by H.E. Bates. The book was published in 1958, but it spawned a much-loved British television series in the early 1990s.

It is not surprising that a tree with so many mystical properties and connections attracted note as a medicine. Seventeenth-century herbalist Nicholas Culpeper described the medicinal properties of the hawthorn as he knew them:

> It is a tree of Mars. The seeds in the berries beaten to powder being drank in wine, are held singularly good against the stone [= e.g. kidney stones], and are good for the dropsy [= fluid retention]. The distilled water of the flowers stay the lask [= diarrhoea]. The seed cleared from the down, bruised and boiled in wine, and drank, is good for inward tormenting pains. If cloths or sponges be wet in the distilled water, and applied to any place wherein thorns and splinters, or the like,

The top of the maypole is traditionally decorated with flowers including hawthorn or 'may'.

do abide in the flesh, it will notably draw them forth. And thus you see the thorn gives a medicine for its own pricking, and so doth almost everything else.

For many centuries, hawthorns have had a very practical use in rural areas: constituting a major part of the hedgerows that divide the land. Their impenetrable tangling branches and spines make them a superb barrier to prevent livestock wandering and to impede trespassers. They are also ideal retreats for many kinds of wildlife from nesting birds, to small mammals, to insects. The value of this role as a natural fence seems to have been known since Anglo-Saxon times because the tree's name means 'hedge thorn' and is mentioned in ninth- and tenth-century texts such as the Lindisfarne Gospels. By the fifteenth century, hawthorns had become an integral component of 'quickset' hedges – created by planting cuttings of young trees directly into the ground. Other trees were suitable too, but some were not favoured, as agriculturalist Arthur Standish wrote in 1612 when describing how to create a quickset hedge:

Hawthorn hedges are a longstanding feature of the British countryside and are still common today; they are important retreats for wildlife.

> Take whitethorn, crab tree, hollin mixed together – or else any one of them, and by no means, if you can chuse, set any blackthorne [= sloes] among them for that it will grow into the fields ward and spoyle pasture and tear the wool off the sheepe's back.

Finally, in terms of our language, the importance of the hawthorn in English place names should not be overlooked: Thornhill, Thorne, Thornton, Thornbury, and so on. A significant example in history was Thorney Island, which was once a secluded area just off the river Thames, London, where Edward the Confessor built a church amongst the hawthorns. That church has long since gone and was replaced by a far more grand building in the thirteenth century, which bears the more familiar name of the location today – Westminster Abbey.

Long-term forecast

If the hawthorn produced a particular abundance of its red berries or 'haws' then traditionally this foretold a harsh winter. The extra provision of haws was said to be God's method of trying to protect his creatures, especially songbirds, from starvation during the icy months ahead.

Hawthorn berries or 'haws'.

Hazel

Catkins.

*T*he name of this tree dates to Anglo-Saxon times when it was referred to by words such as *haesel* or *haesl*. The native hazel (*Corylus avellana*) was economically important in the Middle Ages, having long been prized for its timber as well as its nuts. The lengthy, dangling catkins have attracted many alternative names such as lambs' tails or cats' tails, and were regarded as a sign that winter was ending and spring was on the way: 'the voice of promise, and the herald of hope'.

Hazel trees are commonly pollarded, which involves removing the upper limbs of the tree to encourage a dense growth of new thin branches. Hazels are also coppiced – that is, the tree is cut down to near ground level to promote growth of new branches from the stump. Both processes encourage the production of numerous slim, vertical branches that can be regularly harvested. These pruning processes result in rather short shrub-like trees, which is the characteristic appearance of many hazels even today.

The speedily generated young hazel branches found use as poles, walking sticks, fishing rods, handles, hoops and so forth. Importantly, the thin new growth of hazel branches was tough and pliable and was woven, like willow, to make sturdy baskets and crates. It was employed in the wattle and daub style of building construction. In

Coppiced hazel in a bluebell wood.

this, a latticework of long interweaving branches (the wattle) was infilled with clay or mud (the daub). Almost any kind of timber might be adopted to produce this type of material, but hazel poles grow quickly and are comparatively strong. They were also woven into fence panels called hurdles, which were needed to construct livestock pens, to divide up fields and gardens, as windbreaks, to strengthen riverbanks, and even to make the jumps for equestrian events.

Small chips of hazel wood were found to purify wine, and when thin hazel branches were turned to charcoal they made conveniently shaped sketching crayons for artists who would mark out a composition in black outline before beginning to paint.

The name for the fruit of the hazel tree can cause confusion because a range of different words have existed side by side for centuries. The archaic 'hedge nut' was familiar in Tudor times, but three other terms have persisted to the modern day: hazelnut, filbert, and cobnut, and they can be interpreted differently. There was confusion over the precise meaning of these words historically, and it persists to some extent to this day, with individuals having their own preferred meanings, although 'hazelnut' is now overwhelmingly the most common term.

The most generic name – and indeed the oldest – is 'hazelnut', which was in use as far back as the eighth century. It may refer to the nut from any variety of hazel tree, wild

Wild hazelnuts or cobnuts.

or cultivated, but in modern UK parlance it tends to describe the dried, cultivated nuts sold in shops. The two other names, filbert and cobnut, both seem to have come into English in medieval times, although the former appears to be the older word. Filbert is believed to be a corruption of the name of a prominent French monk and later saint, Philibert of Jumièges, since the nuts ripen around the time of his feast day (20 August). So this term may have been introduced by the Normans and usually signified cultivated hazelnuts, as opposed to wild ones. These days in the UK, filbert is an uncommon word that – if used at all – is often reserved for the more elongated nuts from a non-native species of hazel known as the filbert tree (*Corylus maxima*).

The word 'cobnut' often denotes wild hazelnuts picked and eaten while fresh and not left to dry, but it has also long been associated with certain varieties of round, cultivated hazelnuts grown especially in Kent and the surrounding areas. These cultivated nuts are larger than wild varieties. Interestingly, cobnut was the name of a game that was played by children for centuries, although it seems to have had a number of variations. The antiquarian James Halliwell described the game as he understood it in 1846:

> Cob-nut. A game which consists in pitching at a row of nuts piled up in heaps of four, three at the bottom and one at the top of each heap. All the nuts knocked down are the property of the pitcher. The nut used for pitching is called the *cob*.

It's important to harvest hazelnuts before the squirrels tuck in.

It is sometimes played on the top of a hat with two nuts, when one tries to break the nut of the other with his own, or with two rows of hazel nuts strung on strings through holes bored in the middle.

Although wild hazelnuts have long been an important source of food, it is vital not to wait too long before harvesting them. Anyone with a hazel in their garden will know how voraciously grey squirrels tuck in, quickly devouring every single nut on the tree. Before the arrival of the grey squirrel from North America, it was the native red squirrel, as well as mice and dormice that robbed the nuts. Abraham Cowley was an important seventeenth-century poet, and aptly describes the behaviour of squirrels in his poem *Pomona*:

> *The Hazel with light Forces marches up,*
> *The first in field, upon whose Nutty top*
> *A Squirrel sits, and wants no other shade*
> *Than what by his own spreading Tail is made;*
> *He culls the soundest, dextrously picks out*
> *The Kernels sweet and throws the Shells about.*

Hazel was supposed to have various magical properties. For example, hazelnuts could predict the identity of a sweetheart. Nuts were each given the name of a potential admirer and then placed at the edge of a hot fire. The hazelnut that burst with the loudest bang or burned the brightest revealed the identity of your true love. In some parts of the UK it was so customary to enjoy this activity on Halloween that 31 October was alternatively known as Nutcrack Night. The eighteenth-century poet John Gay was well aware of the custom and described it in *The Shepherd's Week*:

> *Two hazel-nuts I threw into the flame,*
> *And to each nut I gave a sweet-heart's name.*
> *This with the loudest bounce me sore amazed,*
> *That in a flame of brightest colour blazed.*
> *As blazed the nut, so may thy passion grow,*
> *For 'twas thy nut that did so brightly glow.*

Hazel nuts were seen as a symbol of fruitfulness, and various old superstitions suggested an association between the extent of the nut harvest and the likelihood that local women would give birth. A year abundant in nuts would ensure a large number of babies.

Another example of the peculiarly mystical properties of hazel comes from it being the conventional wood from which dowsing or divination rods were made. These days, dowsing is associated with looking for underground water, and the rods are made of all sorts of material, but in ages past it was a method for detecting a whole range of things, as seventeenth-century writer John Evelyn explains:

The use of the hazel… for riding switches [= whips] and divinatory rods for the detecting and finding of minerals (at least, if that tradition be no imposture) is very wonderful; by whatsoever occult virtue, the forked stick (so cut, and skilfully held) becomes impregnated with those invisible steams and exhalations; as by its spontaneous bending from an horizontal posture, to discover not only mines, and subterraneous treasure and springs of water but criminals guilty of murder etc, made out so solemnly and the effects thereof by the attestation of magistrates and diverse other learned and credible persons (who have critically examined matters of fact) is certainly next to miracle and requires a strong faith.

Some people claimed that certain extraordinary conditions were essential for success when cutting a divining rod from a hazel tree. For example, it had to be performed after sunset and before sunrise, and only on certain nights, among which were Good Friday, Epiphany, Shrove Friday, St John's Day, and the first night of a new moon or the one preceding it. In the actual process of cutting, you had to face east, from where the first rays of the morning sun came, or the rod would be valueless. The best magic wands used by sorcerers and magicians were claimed to come from hazel as well, and the Roman god Mercury's hazel wand was supposed to have bestowed learning on the ancients.

Apart from their more magical uses, the nuts of the hazel tree, more than any other part, seem to have attracted a quite wide array of disparate medicinal uses. The Tudor herbalist John Gerard offered this description:

Water divining or dowsing was traditionally practised using a long thin branch, split part-way, and hazel was a popular tree from which to take it. Image from *A Tour in Wales* by Thomas Pennant (1726–98). (*Courtesy of National Library of Wales*)

Hazel nuts newly gathered, and not as yet dry, contain in them a certain superfluous moisture, by reason whereof they are windy: not only the new gathered nuts, but the dry also, be very hard of digestion for they are of an earthy and cold essence, and of a hard and sound substance, for which cause also they very slowly pass through the belly. Therefore they are troublesome and clogging to the stomach, cause headache, especially when they be eaten in too great a quantity.

The kernels of nuts made into milk, like almonds, do mightily bind the belly and are good for the lask [= diarrhoea] and the bloody flux [= dysentery].

The same doth cool exceedingly in hot fevers and burning agues.

Hazel leaf in autumn.

However, Jacobean herbalist Nicolas Culpeper attributes some quite different curative properties to the hazelnut. He states their value for coughs, colds, and to stop women's monthly menstrual bleeds. He writes what might be called a rather engaging rant about the reputed ill effects of hazelnuts on the chest:

Why should the vulgar so familiarly affirm, that eating nuts causes shortness of breath, than which nothing is false? For, how can that which strengthens the lungs, cause shortness of breath? I confess, the opinion is far older than I am; I knew tradition was a friend to error before, but never that he was the father of slander. Or are men's tongues so given to slander one another, that they must slander nuts too, to keep their tongues in use? If any part of the hazel nut be stopping [= obstructive], it is the husks and shells, and no one is so mad as to eat them unless physically [= medically required]; and the red skin which covers the kernel, you may easily pull off. And so thus have I made an apology for nuts, which cannot speak for themselves.

Holly

*T*he name of this tree is ancient, although the modern word has altered a little from the Anglo-Saxon *holen*. It was sometimes called the *holme*, or even the *hulver* – the latter being derived from its Norse name *hulfr*. It is an evergreen native British tree that often has a relatively low-lying shrubby habit. However, in the right situations holly can form a freestanding tree of reasonable size, although this takes a considerable time because it grows slowly. It is an attractive tree, providing year-round colour, and this has always made it popular. The Scottish garden designer Walter Nicol summed up the views of many when he wrote in 1812:

> There is something so extremely cheerful in the holly, particularly late in autumn and in winter, that, wherever it appears, it never fails to command attention and to please.

For centuries, holly has been planted as an attractive hedge to divide up land, provide shelter from the wind, and to prevent trespass. Its densely packed spiky leaves make a virtually impenetrable barrier and it can grow to a considerable height. The seventeenth-

If properly cared for and regularly clipped, holly can form a high and dense hedge as good as any fence or wall for ensuring privacy and deterring intruders.

century diarist John Evelyn described seeing such hedges 20 feet high, and was very proud of his own large holly hedge at his house, Say's Court, in Deptford. He planted it following a recommendation from Russian tsar Peter the Great, who once stayed with him:

> Is there under heaven a more glorious and refreshing object of the kind than an impregnable hedge, of about four hundred feet in length, nine feet high, and five in diameter, which I can show in my new raised gardens at Say's Court (thanks to the Czar of Muscovy) at any time of the year, glittering with its armed and varnished leaves, the taller standards at orderly distances, blushing with their natural coral.

A number of plants are associated with Christmas. There is the Christmas tree itself, of course, as well as mistletoe and poinsettias, but holly has been linked to festive celebrations for longer than any of them. Even today, wreaths of holly adorn doors and houses, and the leaves and berries are frequently part of the decoration on Christmas cards. Depictions of Father Christmas in Victorian and Edwardian times commonly showed him with a holly crown. The usual explanation for this link with Christmas is that it was a pagan custom taken up by the early church, which often adopted pre-Christian traditions to show converts that longstanding habits would not have to be abandoned by accepting God.

Father Christmas and his holly crown in 1836 (left) and in about 1900 (right).

The Romans, for example, honoured the god Saturn in mid–December with a festival called Saturnalia, which involved an uninhibited public celebration and feasting that extended to all levels of society. Boughs of holly were sent as gifts, symbolising good will, as part of this festival. The British population would have been exposed to Roman religious practices such as these over more than four centuries of rule. However, it has also been conjectured that the ancient druids may have revered holly as a tree that was green and bore fruit during the dark and cold winter months and was thus a symbol of rebirth and the hope of better days to come. After all, its evergreen nature, spiky leaves, and blood-red berries made it stand out – a tree like no other. The Romans bestowed magical properties upon it: Pliny states that holly will deflect witchcraft and protect against being struck by lightning. The Christmas carol *The Holly and the Ivy* dates to at least the early nineteenth century but may be older, and it, too, marks the holly as special:

Holly saplings are very tenacious – they will grow in unusual locations and withstand harsh conditions that many other young trees cannot tolerate.

Bird-catching tree

The bark of the holly tree was once used to make a substance called birdlime. The bark was boiled for twelve hours, then allowed to ferment for a fortnight before being pounded in a mortar. This created a glue-like consistency to which some oil was finally added.

Birdlime was one method for catching birds – either to eat or for selling as pets. Typically, food was set as bait, and sticky birdlime was smeared onto sticks or perches nearby. Birds soon became trapped and were unable to escape, enabling the human hunter to retrieve them. It was formerly a very widespread practice, but is cruel and now illegal in the UK. Birdlime was applied in a similar manner to stop pests including birds, rodents, and insects from eating garden crops.

The Elizabethan herbalist John Gerard stated that birdlime was poisonous because if eaten 'it glueth up all the entrails, it shutteth and draweth together the guts and passages of excrements, and by this means it bringeth destruction to man'.

The Cockney expression 'doing bird' means going to prison, and is believed to be rhyming slang: 'doing time' rhymes with 'birdlime'.

Densely packed holly berries in autumn are a good food source for birds such as thrushes. This picture was taken near the top of a tree, where leaves can be less spiky presumably because they are unlikely to be browsed by herbivores and so don't need as much protection.

The holly and the ivy,
When they are both full grown
Of all the trees that are in the wood
The holly bears the crown

This carol makes repeated connections between the holly and Christ – the prickly leaves being reminiscent of the crown of thorns worn at the crucifixion, and the red berries symbolising drops of his blood. Of course, the name holly tree is very reminiscent of 'holy tree', and witches were reputed to detest it for this reason.

There was a certain amount of mysticism associated with holly, and many odd beliefs and customs associated with it. In the Victorian era, the author Richard Folkard collected together many of these old folklore tales. Here is one that he related about holly:

In Northumberland, holly is employed in a form of divination. There the prickly variety is called he-holly, and the smooth, she-holly. It is the leaves of the latter only that are deemed proper for divining purposes. These smooth leaves must be plucked late on a Friday, by persons careful to preserve an unbroken silence from the time they go out to the dawn of the following morn. The leaves must

Although often thought of as a small tree or shrub, holly can grow to a tree of considerable size in the right conditions.

be collected in a three-cornered handkerchief, and on being brought home, nine of them must be selected, tied with nine knots into the handkerchief, and placed beneath the pillow. Then, sleep being obtained, dreams worthy of all credit will attend this rite.

The timber of holly is particularly white and hard and is commonly compared in colour to ivory. The wood has sometimes been chosen to provide decoration by cabinetmakers: providing inlays and marquetry details. However, it is a very 'wet' wood and takes a long time to dry properly so it is inclined to crack; it has also been a comparatively expensive wood because it grows slowly and trees large enough to fell for woodworking purposes are not common. Interestingly, its fine grain meant that it was often stained black to form a more affordable substitute for ebony.

Medicinally, a solution made from holly bark was once promoted to treat coughs, and poultices soaked in it were recommended to help the healing of broken bones. The poisonous berries were sometimes employed to make people sick when a physician deemed it an appropriate treatment, and holly was additionally advised to treat colic or dysentery. John Pechey wrote in 1694: 'The prickles of the leaves boyl'd in posset-drink, wonderfully ease the cholick, and pains in the bowels. With this, a gentlewoman cured herself and many others, when other medicines would do no good.'

A stand of hornbeam saplings.

Hornbeam

*T*he hornbeam caused our ancestors some confusion. For many centuries, no one could decide what kind of tree it was: hornbeam was variously allied to the birches and even the maples. In many parts of Britain it was said to be from the elm family and one old name for the hornbeam was the yoke-elm, since the wood was traditionally used to make the yoke for oxen to pull the plough. However, more commonly the hornbeam was said to be a type of beech tree, since the leaves do have a superficial similarity. In former times it was sometimes known as the horn-beech, particularly in south-east England where it was, and is, most common.

In fact, the hornbeam is a member of the birch family and its scientific name is *Carpinus betulus*, the word *betula* being the Latin term for birch.

The name hornbeam comes from the Anglo-Saxon word for tree, *béam*, and the prefixed 'horn' is supposed to allude to the hard, horny texture of the wood. John Gerard described the unusual properties of the wood in his Herbal of 1597:

> The wood or timber whereof is better for arrows and shafts, pulleys for mills and such like devices than elm or witch-hazel. For in time it waxeth so hard that the toughness and hardness of it may be rather compared to horn than unto wood, and therefore it was called horne-beam or hard-beam.

Early nineteenth-century botanist John Claudius Loudon also attested to the strength of the timber:

Hornbeam leaves resemble beech leaves.

It is exceedingly strong. A piece 2 inches square and 7 feet 8 inches long having supported 228lb, while a similar beam of ash broke under 200lb; one of birch under 190lb; of oak 185lb; of beech 165lb; and of all other woods very much less.

Because of its strength, it was favoured in situations where durability was required such as mill cogs, wheels, piano hammers, chopping blocks, and handles. However, it was not the easiest wood to work because it was so hard that it quickly blunted the carpenter's tools; moreover, it had a complex grain and was inclined to splinter.

Despite being described by ancient writers, and being a native British tree, the hornbeam seems to have attracted very little attention in terms of folklore and was not considered important medicinally. It was not frequently planted as an ornamental tree either, but the hornbeam did find great favour as a hedge. These were used from medieval times onwards to break up a garden into compartments, and to form decorative arcades, bowers and alcoves, and even to construct mazes. Hornbeams were sometimes planted to act as a 'nursery hedge': to protect tender plants and saplings from the wind and winter frosts.

Hornbeam yields a pale wood that was difficult to work before the invention of power tools because it is so hard, and mature trees often have an awkward grain.

John Evelyn extolled the virtues of the hornbeam hedge most eloquently in his book *Silva*, published in 1664:

> It makes the noblest and the stateliest hedges for long walks in gardens or parks of any tree whatsoever whose leaves are deciduous, and forsake their branches in winter, because it grows tall and so sturdy as not to be wronged by the winds. Besides it will furnish [leaves] to the very foot of the stem, and flourishes with a glossy and polished verdure which is exceeding delightful, of long continuance, and of all other the harder woods, the speediest grower.

Evelyn goes on to remark that the royal hornbeam hedges at Hampton Court were maintained to 15 or 20 feet high.

Later in the same book, Evelyn complained that although hornbeams were more resilient to damage by deer than almost any other species, mature trees were often hacked about by foresters and this either killed or deformed them. This was probably because a great deal of hornbeam timber was burned as fuel or used to produce charcoal, and mature trees were pollarded to provide the wood required.

A modern hornbeam hedge.

A mature hornbeam tree.

The characteristic fruits of the hornbeam.

By contrast, another famous figure loved the hornbeams precisely because they were so deformed and knobbly. William Morris, the celebrated designer and activist, was outraged that Victorian developers sought to destroy Epping Forest on the edge of Greater London where he grew up. One of the area's dominant trees was the hornbeam and the former royal forest had already been much reduced in size. In 1895, Morris wrote the first of a series of public letters to the *Daily Chronicle*, which contained these words:

> I venture to ask you to allow me a few words on the subject of the present

treatment of Epping Forrest… The special character of it was derived from the fact that by far the greater part was a wood of hornbeams, a tree not common save in Essex and Herts. It was certainly the biggest hornbeam wood in these islands, and I suppose in the world. The said hornbeams were all pollards, being shrouded every four to six years, and were interspersed in many places with holly thickets; and the result was a very curious and characteristic wood, such as can be seen nowhere else. And I submit that no treatment of it can be tolerable which does not maintain the hornbeam wood intact.

In the end, the campaign by Morris and others was to prove successful and the forest was not destroyed. Epping Forest stands today, covers nearly 6,000 acres, and still contains a large number of hornbeams and over 50,000 ancient trees of various species.

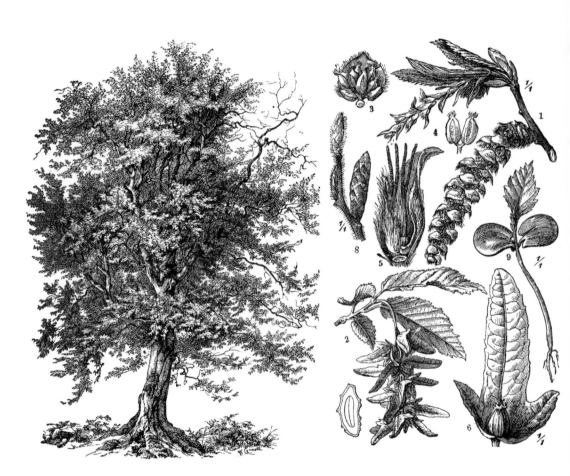

Nineteenth-century botanical illustration of the hornbeam.

Horse
Chestnut

Avenue of horse chestnuts.

*T*he horse chestnut is not native to the UK, and is unrelated to the sweet chestnut. It was introduced in the sixteenth or seventeenth century as an ornamental tree, and for this purpose it has proved very popular to judge by the large numbers of them that exist. There are few trees in the UK that have such magnificent flowers: laburnum and magnolia being perhaps its commonest rivals. The familiar seeds, or conkers, lend the tree its other common title of 'conker tree'.

The beautiful flower of the horse chestnut.

The biggest mystery is the tree's name: why the *horse* chestnut? There have been several theories over the centuries. A frequent explanation has been that the tree came to Europe from the Ottoman Empire, and the Turks reputedly ground up conkers and mixed them with the regular food given to their horses. Another very plausible reason is that when the leaves fall off the tree they leave a horseshoe-shaped scar. Others have suggested that the name was coined derisively: conkers look superficially like sweet chestnuts but they are inedible as far as humans are concerned, and so might be considered 'only fit for horses'. In the nineteenth century, it was often stated that the name was derived from the practice of administering conkers to horses for relieving ailments such as cough.

The horse chestnut tree has had no important practical uses. The conkers are eaten by deer, and have been crushed to add to the feeds of sheep, cows and poultry. Pigs apparently do not like them. They contain a mild soap and can be used for washing by just mashing them up, and they also have an additional mild bleaching action. In the eighteenth century particularly, much effort was put into trying to find a commercial use for conkers, especially in France. Entrepreneurs, inventors, scientists and manufacturers felt sure that there must be some value to conkers and investigated them from every

Record-breaking conker

Having had only a few centuries for early pioneers to reach massive size, it is no surprise that there are few very large 'conker' trees in the UK. However, the record for the largest specimen is held by one in the grounds of Hughenden Manor in Buckinghamshire. This was once the estate of Prime Minister Benjamin Disraeli, although the tree long predates his tenure. It was planted over 300 hundred years ago, and in 2014, an official measurement of its girth showed it had attained 7.33 metres.

Horse chestnut seed in its spiky shell.

angle. Numerous schemes and ideas were explored at great length and expense. But all to no avail. One commentator wrote:

> Of all the waste substances which might be profitably employed in domestic economy, there is none which has given rise to more discussion or on which so many attempts have been made as the fruit of the horse chestnut… At various periods the utilisation of this product has attracted public attention, and many speculators have essayed to make it an object of commerce.

Perhaps not wanting to admit defeat, the French decided that conkers might be suited to the washing of yarn, and that was about the sum total of the benefits they discovered. There was one small, modestly successful commercial use in the UK. Conkers comprise mostly of carbohydrate and in 1776, Lord William Murray, then Lord Chief Justice, obtained a patent for extracting starch from them. His process was to peel then grate them, and then wash the pulp before baking and drying it.

The timber of the horse chestnut is soft and lacks tannin or resin so it is easily damaged and rots quickly, hence it has rarely been utilised historically except when other better sources of timber were in short supply. Even then, it was only considered fit for low-value utility items such as roughly worked boxes and crates.

However, the horse chestnut has contributed a small benefit to the lives of schoolchildren since at least early Victorian times – the game of conkers. The name

Horse chestnut seeds or conkers.

possibly comes from the verb 'conquer', and seems to have been based on an older game that involved knocking snail shells together. Two opponents face each other with a conker threaded on to a length of string or a bootlace. They take it in turns to swipe at each other's dangling conker until one is smashed. Various means were traditionally available to create a harder conker that was more likely to win, including baking them, soaking them in vinegar, or storing them somewhere warm to dry out. There were a number of variations on the basic rules: for example, if the strings become entangled during combat, the first to shout 'strings' had an extra free hit of their opponent. A conker that had defeated two others became a 'twicer'; if another twicer defeated it then the victory tallies could be added together to create a 'fourer' and so on. In this way, some conkers could accumulate quite magnificent totals.

Lime

*T*here are three native lime trees in the UK: the large-leaved lime, the small-leaved lime and the third, known as the common lime, is a hybrid of the two species that occurs in the wild. The original Anglo-Saxon name for the tree was *lind*, meaning shield, from which the tree gets its alternative title of the linden tree. Lind was the predominant name until the seventeenth century, when the new version 'lime' started to appear in print – presumably derived from its predecessor – and from this point the word lind began to disappear.

The fact that lime wood was used to make shields is well established, being a wood that the Romans were known to use for the purpose. Lime wood shields are referred to more than once in *Beowulf*, and it is mentioned in an Anglo-Saxon poem, believed to have been recited as a charm to help cure rheumatism:

> *I stood under lime wood, under a light shield,*
> *Where the mighty women gathered their power*
> *And screaming, sent forth their spears.*

Lime wood is disinclined to split after being struck by, say, a spear, and tends to absorb the power of impact. It is also not too heavy. These were good properties for a shield.

Characteristic bright green leaves of the lime in spring.

Lime wood is light in colour, easy to work, and not liable to warp so in former times it was employed for a whole variety of roles other than shield–making. In the seventeenth and eighteenth centuries it was widely taken up in the construction of items as diverse as domestic utensils, window lattices, chopping blocks, piano keys, ornamental boxes, architectural models and building templates, and ships' pumps amongst many others. Given its general usefulness, the seventeenth-century author John Evelyn railed against the fact that lime wood was commonly imported into the UK from the Netherlands at great cost. 'It is a shameful negligence,' he said 'that we are no better provided of nurseries of a tree so choice, and universally acceptable.'

The soft nature of lime wood, its uniform colour, and freedom from knots earned it the name of the 'carver's tree', and with good reason. Lime has been widely used for carving figures, toys, statues, and bas–relief images, and in these roles it was rated superior to any other British native tree. One carver in particular brought the working of lime wood to an apex. His name was Grinling Gibbons, and during the late seventeenth and early eighteenth centuries he became famous for creating the most elaborate and beautiful carvings from lime wood. Gibbons' carvings still adorn the interior of St Paul's Cathedral and several other London churches, as well as Kensington Palace, Trinity College Cambridge, Petworth House in Sussex, and many others. The intricacy of some of his work, created centuries before electric tools, must be seen to be believed.

A lime tree avenue.

By the seventeenth century, the deliberate planting of lime trees as part of landscape and town design began to become popular. This development was egged on by the redoubtable John Evelyn, who even reputedly persuaded the King to plant some limes in St James's Park in London. Evelyn waxed lyrical on the subject:

> Is there a more ravishing or delightful object, then to behold some entire streets and whole towns planted with these trees in even lines before their doors, so as they seem like cities in a wood? This is extremely fresh, of admirable effect against the epilepsy for which the delicately scented blossoms are held prevalent, and screen the houses both from winds, sun, and dust.

As landscape adornments, these trees had a number of advantages: they grew quickly, attained a large size, were sturdy and upright with a single trunk, and bestowed great shade. The bright, almost fluorescent green colour of the young leaves was often admired, as were the flowers so beloved of insects, with their sweet smell. Other advantages claimed for the lime tree were that it seemed more storm resistant than many other trees; that it was relatively tolerant of urban pollution; and that it tended to age gracefully without dropping branches or becoming hollow. It became fashionable to plant lime trees on estates, and in parks and towns; avenues of them were especially in vogue for the next 300 years or so.

The Scottish garden designer Walter Nicol advocated the lime tree avenue. In 1810, shortly before his death, he wrote:

> The lime is to be found as a standard, or as an avenue tree, about most residences of note in the kingdom… Perhaps no tree is better adapted to the formation of an avenue or a walk near a residence. Indeed, it has been preferred for these purposes, by common consent, for more than a hundred years back.

Many of these lime avenues are still standing and have become well known, but perhaps the most famous – certainly the largest – is the avenue of common limes at Clumber Park, Nottinghamshire. It was planted in about 1840 by artist and garden designer William S. Gilpin for the Duke of Newcastle. It now consists of 1,296 trees, and is an impressive 2 miles long. Large tree avenues were a confident declaration of wealth and status, created interest in what might otherwise be a flat landscape, and acted as an imposing conduit to the owner's residence.

There were some quite surprising uses for lime tree products other than the timber. The bark, for example, was an article of commerce. The tall trunks of the trees are free of side branches and so the bark can be stripped off in long pieces. These were soaked in water, and then macerated, before being divided into narrow fibrous slips called lime bast. This formed the basis of a weaving industry, with bast being made into ropes, mats, and baskets; in some Bronze Age cultures it was even made into clothing. In 1838, John Loudon noted that this practice was still ongoing in Cornwall and Devon at the time; in other parts of Europe, the bast was used to make a crude fabric for sacks, and even nets.

Lime trees can grow to a lofty height if not pollarded, even in towns; this one dwarfs the three-storey building next to it and stands at about 90 feet.

Fruits of the lime tree.

Lime tree honey was highly prized too and sold for a higher price than other kinds, and the sap of the lime could also be treated to make sugar. It was even claimed in eighteenth-century Prussia that the fruits of the lime tree could be manufactured into a substance remarkably like chocolate, but it did not keep well. The leaves were fed to cattle, fresh or dried, and the aromatic lime tree flowers were desiccated to make a soothing herbal tea in the Second World War.

Lime trees are not especially renowned for their medicinal properties. Tudor herbalist John Gerard acclaimed the tree's flowers as a treatment for pains in the head 'of a cold cause', dizziness, apoplexy, and epilepsy; another recommendation was to boil the leaves and mix them with hogs' grease and other ingredients to treat boils. Nicholas Culpeper advocated a 'mucilaginous liquor' prepared from lime tree buds as being particularly agreeable to patients with fever or kidney stones. Seventeenth-century authors such as

What's in a name?

Carl Linnaeus was the Swedish zoologist who formalised the system of Latin names for animals and plant species. However, his own name is derived from the Swedish word for lime tree, having been chosen by his father because of a large specimen that grew in his garden.

'Limeys' is the old US name for people from the UK, but has nothing to do with the lime tree. It arose because British sailors used to drink lime juice to stop them getting scurvy.

John Pechey suggested that the fruits cured dysentery, and when stuffed up the nose with vinegar they stopped it bleeding! A mucilage made from the bark was applied to burns and wounds.

Not a lime in leaf, but a winter tree covered in mistletoe. Older lime trees are one of the commonest homes for this parasitic plant, its growth becoming most obvious in the winter months after the trees have lost their leaves.

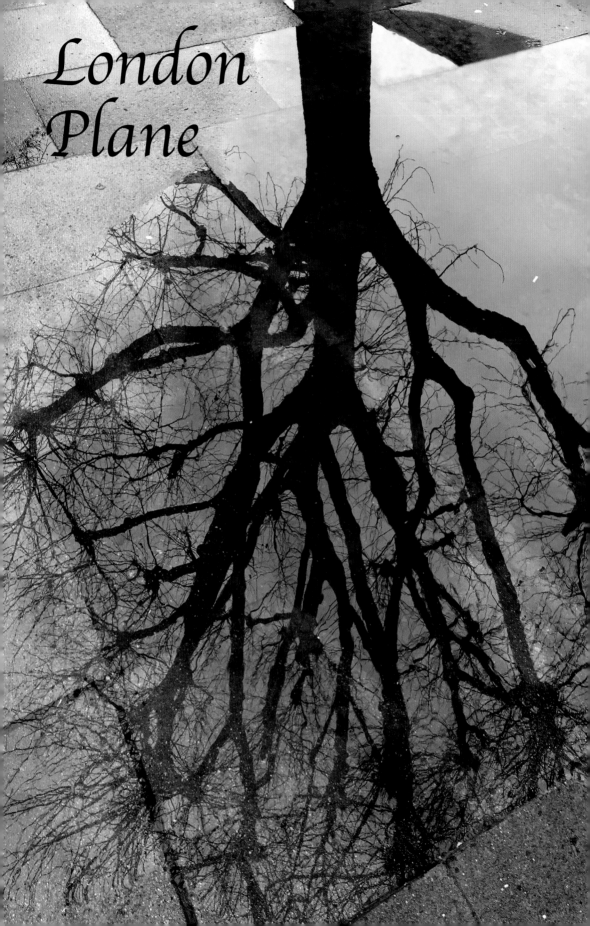

London
Plane

*T*he London plane is the only plane tree found in the UK in appreciable quantity. It is a very common tree because it is especially suited to life in an urban environment and so provides the greenery in numerous city centres. London planes form a backdrop to many of the capital's most famous tourist attractions: they line the Mall leading to Buckingham Palace, flank the entrance to St Paul's Cathedral, stand guard near the Tower of London, and watch over Parliament.

Yet the London plane does not occur naturally in the wild. It is a hybrid between two other species – the Oriental plane (*Platanus orientalis*) and the American sycamore (*Platanus occidentalis*). This hybridisation would not have occurred without human intervention because the parent species grow on separate continents – the Oriental plane is from eastern Europe and Asia, whilst the American sycamore is native to North America. In the mid-seventeenth century, plants were sought from all over the world and brought back to Europe, and these two species of tree began to grow in close proximity in the gardens of plant collectors. The hybrid was soon noted and is now called the London plane (*Platanus × acerifolia*) since it has been so widely planted in the city – it is estimated that it accounts for at least half of the trees in central London.

However, the London plane is commonly selected to grow in cities all over the world – from Birmingham to New York to Sydney. Besides its attractive foliage, bark and fruits, it has many features that make it well adapted to survival in an urban environment. It is a tall tree that provides ample shade in summer and, as one Victorian enthusiast noted, it is important that any urban tree can grow high enough so that their lower branches do not interfere with vehicles passing underneath them. The London plane achieves this height very satisfactorily, but if it grows too large it can be quite harshly pollarded without dying, and it still maintains an attractive shape when it regrows. It will endure considerable heat and a moderate amount of drought; yet it is able to withstand freezing winters and compacted soil as well. Finally, and most importantly, the London plane is not only tolerant of city pollution, but it will actively remove pollutants from the air – shedding toxins in its leaves and in its bark, which sloughs off in sheets throughout the year.

It is unclear where the London plane first came into being – the two leading potential locations being in Spain or in England. It is possible that hybridisation could have occurred independently in more than one place. In England, the principal site put forward for the tree's genesis is the gardens in Vauxhall belonging to the botanist and plant collector John Tradescant the younger, who certainly had access to specimens of both parents. It was Tradescant who first brought the American sycamore to England in 1636, while the Oriental plane had already been popular in the UK for at least a century. It is a romantic notion that London's most popular tree could also have been born there.

Since the London plane is a relatively new creation, it is not yet known how long it lives, or how large the tree can get. The most ancient trees in the UK are accepted to be the two specimens that were given to Robert Sanderson, Bishop of Lincoln, in the early 1660s; they are still healthy and robust, and can be seen at Buckden Towers in Cambridgeshire. The oldest tree in London is at Barn Elms and dates from approximately

Regular pollarding of London planes restricts their height but new growth occurs readily from the crown in the form of multiple small branches. This provides a different but attractive shape.

The London plane fits into all sorts of spaces in cities.

London plane trees amongst the tourists near Tower Bridge.

1685, but the oldest in central London are believed to be those in Berkeley Square, which are held to have been planted there in 1789. In terms of size, the London plane generally does not grow over 30 metres in cities, but there are three much more lofty London planes at Bryanston in Dorset planted in 1749 to mark the centenary of the execution of Charles I. The height of one of them was over 49 metres in 2015, making it one of the tallest broadleaved trees of any kind in Europe.

Saucer magnolia about to burst into flower.

Magnolia

*T*he graceful magnolia is a familiar tree in gardens in the UK. Yet it is a primitive flowering plant with an impressively lengthy ancestry: fossilised forebears similar to modern magnolias have been identified from as far back as the Cretaceous period (145 to 66 million years ago).

The magnolia is named after French botanist Pierre Magnol (1638–1715), the man credited with devising plant families: a concept that was to prove so important in systematically classifying every species in the plant kingdom. The many different species of wild magnolia are found in North, Central and South America, and in eastern Asia. This wide geographical distribution of closely related species provides evidence that Asia and America were once joined, during which time the magnolia's ancestors occupied an impressively large area. The plant's flowers allow for pollination by beetles, a method that was clearly highly successful because magnolias have survived to the present day.

The first magnolia grown in the UK was planted by a bishop with a love of gardens. Henry Compton was appointed Bishop of London in 1675, and he shipped out missionaries to the American colonies with instructions to tend to the spiritual needs of the colonists but also to survey the plant life there. When he ordered the Reverend John Bannister to sail for Virginia, he knew he was despatching a man with an equal fascination for the flora of the New World. Accordingly, Bannister sent back to his employer many seeds and cuttings, including some from the sweetbay magnolia (*Magnolia virginiana*).

Nineteenth-century prints of the sweetbay magnolia (*M. virginiana*) on the left, and southern magnolia (*M. grandiflora*) on the right, both natives of North America and the first magnolia trees to be grown in the UK.

Bishop Compton planted the magnolia in his gardens at Fulham Palace in about 1688 and it germinated successfully. The enthusiastic bishop was probably the first to grow many other trees and shrubs from abroad in these gardens including the black walnut and the holm oak.

It was to be over forty years before another magnolia species crossed the Atlantic, and this time it was the southern magnolia (*Magnolia grandiflora*). This, like the sweetbay magnolia, is an evergreen. The first man to grow one in the UK was Sir John Colliton at his house in Exmouth in about 1730. His tree became famous because it was initially the source of all other magnolias of this species grown in the UK: a later owner in the eighteenth century propagated young plants and sold them for as much as five guineas each – a huge sum at the time. Unfortunately, the parent plant was destroyed by mistake in 1794 when a labourer was sent to chop down 'the old apple tree' and instead he took an axe to the magnolia.

It was not until 1780 that the first magnolia reached the UK from Asia. The deciduous yulan magnolia (*Magnolia denudata*) arrived thanks to the efforts of celebrated botanist Sir Joseph Banks, who had sailed with Captain Cook. Banks sent plant hunters all over the world in the eighteenth century and one of the treasures sent home was the yulan magnolia, which was commonly found in the grounds of Buddhist temples in central

The yulan magnolia (*M. denudata*) from China was the first Asian species to be brought to the UK.

A modern variety of the saucer magnolia – 'Alexandrina' (top); and the star magnolia (*M. stellata*) originally from Japan (bottom).

and eastern China. It is still a valued species in China today, and is the official flower of the city of Shanghai. Meanwhile, the native Asian species were to be important to the future of the magnolia in European gardens; other imported Asian species included the purple magnolia (*Magnolia liliiflora*) originally from China, and the star magnolia (*Magnolia stellata*) from Japan.

The commonest magnolia grown in the UK is not a naturally occurring species, but a hybrid. The so-called saucer magnolia was named because its flowers can seem to resemble a cup and saucer. It was created in 1820 by one of Napoleon's cavalry officers after his retirement from the army. Étienne Soulange-Bodin had studied botany and he cross-bred two Asian magnolias – the yulan magnolia and the purple magnolia – to create a hybrid with a Latin name in his honour: *Magnolia × soulangeana*. It soon became popular because it was easy to grow, and produced a mass of beautiful large white flowers tinged with pink or purple even on very young trees. By the late 1820s the saucer magnolia had been introduced to the UK: it was widely admired and quickly became fashionable. Since that time many varieties have been developed.

Magnolia grandiflora remains a popular plant in its native USA, especially in the southern states where it is something of an iconic plant. Both Louisiana and Mississippi have adopted it as their state flower, and the plant is so common in Mississippi that it is officially nicknamed The Magnolia State. A play called *Steel Magnolias* by Robert Harling is set in Louisiana and became a successful film in 1989. It concerns a group of women in a small southern town who at times are fragile like flowers, but they are also tough when they need to be.

Magnolia grandiflora in bloom.

Maple

Japanese maple.

Maple is a name with Anglo-Saxon origins, and its antiquity is borne out by it being part of English place names in the Domesday Book, such as Mappleton in Yorkshire. Although there are a large number of maple species, the only one native to the UK is the field maple (*Acer campestre*) – sometimes called the common, hedge, small-leaved, or lesser maple by our ancestors.

Like hawthorn, the field maple is a small tree that sometimes grows to a reasonable size as an isolated specimen but is more often seen as part of a hedgerow. The eighteenth-century artist William Gilpin initially appeared to be dismissive of it: 'We seldom see it employed in any nobler service than in filling up its part in a hedge in company with thorns, briars, and other ditch trumpery.' However, he goes on to state that 'In the few instances I have met with this tree in a state of maturity, its form has appeared picturesque.' This was high praise indeed, because Gilpin is generally credited as popularising *picturesque* as an artistic term that he defined as a 'kind of beauty which is

A mature field maple like this one is still a fairly small tree.

agreeable in a picture'. He specifically mentions a large example of a maple tree in the churchyard at Boldre, in the New Forest, and fittingly, perhaps, he chose to be buried beneath this tree when he died in 1804.

However, it is the wood of maple trees that has historically attracted the greatest attention as it is hard, fine-grained, delicately veined, and polishes well. Swellings on the tree and knots in the wood are especially attractive when polished. Various species were prized by the Romans for carving and to make furniture, particularly tables. John Evelyn describes the uses to which maple wood was put in the seventeenth century:

Field maple leaf.

The timber is far superior to beech for all uses of the turner, who seeks it for dishes, cups, trays, trenchers etc.; as the joiner for tables, inlayings, and for the delicateness of the grain when the knurs and nodosities are rarely diapred [= patterned] which does much advance its price. Our turners will work it so thin that it is almost transparent. Also for the lightness employed often by those who make musical instruments.

Maple woods have been used for centuries to make musical instruments; the timber is said to be a tonewood because it conducts sound waves well. Maple is traditionally chosen to make the backs, sides, and necks of stringed instruments such as violins, cellos and double basses, the necks of guitars, and to manufacture harps. Some woodwind instruments and drums have been made from maple as well. The wood is also suited to produce the veneers and marquetry that decorate instruments and furniture. Even the roots of maple were worked if they were large enough. When they contain knots the polished root wood displays beautiful patterns, and it was cut and carved into small items such as snuffboxes, pipes and trinkets.

Maple trees produce large numbers of winged seeds that spiral through the air as they fall; since the twentieth century children have often called them 'helicopters' but other names include 'whirlybirds' and 'maple keys'. The botanical name for the seed is a samara. In the Second World War, the US military developed a container for dropping supplies to isolated troops that was based on the shape of a maple seed. The 'sky hook'

Field maple in winter.

The vibrant autumn leaves of various maple species introduced into the UK: Norway maple (top left); silver maple (top right); red maple (bottom).

could hold 65 pounds of provisions and would spiral down to the ground about its own centre of gravity after being dropped from a plane.

Given its widespread availability it is perhaps surprising that the maple was not credited with more medicinal properties. The Roman writer Pliny claimed it was a good treatment for liver disorders and British herbalists such as Gerard accepted this but offered no further uses. Culpeper described the role of maple: 'The decoction either of the leaves or bark, must needs strengthen the liver much, and so you shall find it to do, if you use it. It is excellently good to open obstructions both of the liver and spleen, and eases pains of the sides thence proceeding.'

In the nineteenth century a variety of species of maple from other countries began to be grown ornamentally on large estates, public parks, and eventually in small private gardens. All maples originate from the northern hemisphere and particularly from North America and eastern Asia. Many varieties of maple – often termed 'acers' in garden centres – are grown for their highly colourful autumn foliage. The native field maple has bright yellow leaves in the autumn, but it cannot compete with the vibrant reds, oranges and golds of many other foreign species. The commonest large introduced species in the UK is the Norway maple from continental Europe and western Asia, but others include the silver maple and red maple from North America. However, perhaps the most popular are the hundreds of cultivars of the Japanese maple, which vary enormously in size, habit, autumn colour and leaf shape. Many of them are small enough to grow in a limited garden space and since the twentieth century they have been widely planted. In Japan itself some miniature versions are even grown as part of the tradition of bonsai.

Sweet taste of success

All maple trees have a sap that is sweet-tasting, but it is the sugar maple (*Acer saccharum*) from Canada and the northern USA that is used for this purpose commercially. These trees are tapped for the sap, which is collected in bulk and then boiled to produce maple syrup; it takes about 40 litres of sap to make 1 litre of maple syrup. Other species of maple can produce a similar syrup but not in sufficient quantity to make it financially worthwhile.

The maple is so intimately associated with Canada that a red leaf features on the nation's flag.

Monkey
Puzzle

Large mature monkey puzzle tree,
probably planted in late Victorian times.

*T*he monkey puzzle tree (*Araucaria auracana*) is an evergreen conifer native to mountainous regions of Chile and Argentina. It is actually the national tree of Chile, where it was in the past felled for timber: its long straight trunks found favour for the production of ships' masts, for example. The monkey puzzle is dioecious – that is, trees are either male or female – and the female tree produces cones that bear seeds, similar in appearance to pine nuts although much larger. These seeds are eaten raw or roasted in South America.

The monkey puzzle is an ancient species – a survivor from the time of the dinosaurs. It was first brought to Europe in 1795 by an enterprising Scottish naval officer and botanist, Archibald Menzies. He was circumnavigating the globe aboard HMS *Discovery* when he was invited to dine with the Governor of Chile at Santiago. As part of the meal, guests were served some interesting large seeds for dessert, and Menzies secretly put some in his pocket. Later, when on board ship, he planted them and they germinated. Five plants endured the journey home to the UK, and Menzies donated three of them

Something of a rarity in the UK these days – a monkey puzzle sapling.

to the Royal Botanic Gardens at Kew. At this stage the tree was known simply as the Chile pine. Unfortunately, only one specimen at Kew lived any length of time, but that one tree survived for nearly a century, dying in 1892.

The wider uptake of monkey puzzle trees had to wait around half a century. An intrepid plant collector from Cornwall, William Lobb, was sent out to Chile by James Veitch, owner of an influential nursey that specialised in obtaining rare plants. Veitch had admired the surviving tree at Kew and knew that he would be on to a winner if he was able to provide his affluent clients with more plants. Consequently, Lobb was instructed to obtain, amongst other things, seeds of the monkey puzzle tree. He sailed to Argentina in 1842 then journeyed overland to the mountainous areas where the trees grew. It was bitterly cold and Lobb frequently fell ill, but he was a determined man. When he eventually found the trees, he managed to shoot the cones down with a shotgun and in this way gathered something like 3,000 seeds.

Returning to England, the seeds were germinated and became a great success – the small seedlings were sold fairly cheaply, but rich landowners paid as much as twenty

The spiky foliage to 'puzzle a monkey'; this female tree bears the ball-shaped growths that are due to become cones.

guineas each for an established sapling. One man who purchased a sapling was Cornish MP Sir William Molesworth. He probably knew about Veitch's impending sale of trees because William Lobb's father, John, was a carpenter on his estate at Pencarrow House. One afternoon Sir William introduced his dinner guests to his new acquisition. One of the party was a well-known barrister named Charles Austin. What happened next varies a little according to source, but Austin marvelled at the sharp foliage and may even have pricked himself on it. Perhaps wondering how on earth any creature could climb up such a spikey tree he said something like 'it would be a puzzle to a monkey'. His friends must have enjoyed the remark, because Austin often related the tale as a witty anecdote in London society and as the Chile pine was then becoming very popular the new name stuck. It was the monkey puzzle pine, the monkey puzzler, and eventually just plain monkey puzzle.

The Victorians and Edwardians loved them and those with enough land commonly planted monkey puzzles in ones and twos as imposing specimen trees. They were exotic status symbols, often established on the lawn near the house so that they could be admired from indoors. Sometimes little thought seems to have been given to the fact that these trees can grow to an enormous size and, sadly, many have been chopped down over the years simply because they became too big to occupy the space they were planted in.

The intricate geometric pattern of monkey puzzle bark is one of its attractive features.

One of the most famous collections of monkey puzzle trees is at Bicton Agricultural College, Budleigh Salterton, Devon. Here, in 1844, James Veitch himself directed the head gardener in creating a monkey puzzle avenue consisting of two rows of twenty-five trees. At 500 metres long, it is the biggest avenue of this species in Europe, and it is still standing. One of the original trees is now over 4 metres in girth and another is around 30 metres tall.

The leathery, spiky leaves of the monkey puzzle tree grow in whorls from the tip of each branch.

Oak

*T*he oak is the commonest woodland tree in England. It is a handsome tree that can live several hundred years; many large, ancient specimens exist and are often admired and cared for. The UK as a whole is often said to be a 'nation of nature lovers', and it is almost impossible to overstate the environmental importance of oaks: they provide shelter and food for countless insects and birds, as well as some mammals and plants. This is an important attribute to a nation filled with ramblers, gardeners, birdwatchers, and devotees of natural history programmes. Fittingly enough, the leaves of the oak are the emblem of the National Trust, and an acorn symbol is used to mark the route of National Trails in England and Wales.

The oak is a tree with many cultural, historical and mythical associations. Its name is an ancient one, written in various forms in the past such as *ac* in Old English and *ooc* or *ake* in medieval times. There are in fact two native species of oak: the much commoner pedunculate oak (*Quercus robur*) is often known as the English oak or common oak, whilst the sessile oak (*Quercus petraea*) is sometimes called the durmast oak or Cornish oak. They are very similar, but there are a number of ways to tell them apart. The leaves of the pedunculate oak are more deeply lobed, for example, and its acorns are borne on long stalks, whereas on the sessile oak the acorns sprout directly from twigs and there are no stalks.

Oak trees provide food and shelter for birds such as the jay, mammals like the grey squirrel, and thousands of insects including the stag beetle.

Acorns on the pedunculate oak.

Until relatively recently, especially as far as timber was concerned, the two trees were collectively referred to simply as 'oak' or 'English oak'. In fact the oak, or more specifically the pedunculate oak, is often asserted as being the national tree of England. The 'Englishness' of the oak tree probably stems from a number of causes. There are many iconic individual trees in England, many of which have historic connections. During the Civil War, Charles II hid from his Parliamentarian pursuers up an oak tree near Boscobel House, Shropshire that became known subsequently as the *Royal Oak* – an event that spawned hundreds of public houses with this name. Robin Hood's merry men supposedly sheltered in an oak tree now called the *Major Oak*, which still stands, and they reputedly hid their food in another tree named *Robin Hood's Larder*, which came down in 1960. *William the Conqueror's Oak* in Windsor Great Park is still standing and alive at the time of writing. It is an ancient tree, and although its age is difficult to estimate, it is unlikely to have been living during the reign of William I. It is probably around 700 years old, but might be older.

It was an oak tree that deflected the arrow that killed the unpopular English king William II. Known as William Rufus because of his red hair, this cruel sovereign with a fiery temper was slain after Sir Walter Tyrell shot an arrow that supposedly ricocheted off an oak and hit the King in the chest, killing him almost instantly. It has often been speculated that this was no accident, but the deliberate assassination of a monarch who was resented within all levels of the populace. Tyrell and the hunting party fled, and the King's body was carried to Winchester in a peasant's cart where it was interred, lamented by few, at the cathedral. His unmarked black tomb can still be seen. When the oak tree involved died, a three-sided stone was erected to mark the spot in the New Forest in 1745. It's now protected by a metal guard, but part of the inscription reads: 'Here stood the oak on which an arrow shot by Sir Walter Tyrell at a stag, glanced and struck King William the Second, surnamed Rufus, in the breast, of which he instantly died, on 2nd August 1100.'

The Conqueror's Oak in Windsor Great Park depicted in the 1870s; it still stands and is probably around 700 years old.

There were many other once-famous oaks named after illustrious people: Harold of Hastings, King Alfred, Geoffrey Chaucer, Edward I, several saints, Queen Anne, Sir Philip Sydney, Oliver Cromwell, Dick Turpin, Alexander Pope and William Wilberforce to name a few. Elizabeth I roamed the country spending a lot of time beneath oak trees, apparently, to judge from all the specimens named after her: she supposedly hunted, dined, sheltered, and was first hailed as queen beneath them.

A number of other English oaks acquired celebrity in the past without a connection to anyone particularly famous. At Burley in the New Forest, there once stood a group of large, ancient oaks, which were especially picturesque, and which were given the name of *The Twelve Apostles*. The *Greendale Oak* at Welbeck, Nottinghamshire was so enormous that an archway was cut through the middle of the living tree in 1724 'higher than the entrance to Westminster Abbey and sufficiently capacious to permit a carriage and four horses to pass through it'. Though ancient and increasingly frail, this tree still survived into the twentieth century. The specimen with the greatest girth ever recorded was the *Cowthorpe Oak* in Yorkshire: in 1804, it measured almost 47 feet! It was so big that forty people could stand together inside its hollow trunk. Such was the importance attached to oaks that the traditional exact centre of England was for centuries marked by the *Midland Oak* near Leamington Spa. This old tree died in the 1950s but has been replaced.

Some of the oak trees of the once-famous *Twelve Apostles* in the New Forest in the early 1800s (above). The centre of England: the *Midland Oak*, near Leamington Spa, in about 1910 (below).

The oak – an old friend?

There is a well-known story that George III leapt from his carriage at Windsor to greet what he thought was an old friend by the roadside. 'There he is!' he cried, handing the reigns to the Queen, and he raced off to meet the man who actually turned out to be a rather large tree. A royal attendant, present at the incident, gave this account in a book published in 1789 probably only a few months after it happened:

> His Majesty now approached a venerable oak that had enlivened the solitude of that quarter of the park upwards of a century and a half. At the distance of a few yards he uncovered [i.e. removed his hat], and advanced, bowing with the utmost respect, and then seizing one of the lower branches, he shook it with the most apparent cordiality and regard – just as a man shakes his friend by the hand. The Queen turned pale with astonishment. The reigns dropped from her hands. Never was I in such consternation…
>
> On my approach, I perceived the King was engaged in earnest conversation… It was the King of Prussia with whom His Majesty enjoyed this rural interview. Continental politics were the subject. What I heard, it would be unpardonable to divulge.

The King sent the poor page away, and it was only by the Queen insisting that she required her husband's company that they were able to persuade him to end this bizarre one-way conversation and return to the carriage. Talking to the oak tree was probably the first significant public incident that heralded the onset of George III's serious mental illness.

Some gnarled old trees have sparked tales of hauntings.

There are – or have been – a particularly large number of celebrated old oaks in England, but there are many in other countries of the UK too. For example, *Merlin's Oak* once stood in Carmarthen, Wales, and there are a number of trees in Scotland that have been named after or associated with the hero William Wallace, all now sadly lost.

Given the gnarled and distorted appearance of elderly oaks, it is no surprise that they have sparked many grisly tales involving individual trees that are often said to have become possessed. Welsh leader Owain Glyndŵr supposedly imprisoned a treacherous rival in a hollow oak tree at Nannau, Meirionnydd, and left him there to die. On his deathbed in 1415, tradition has it that the remorseful Glyndŵr confessed, and only then was the skeleton of his enemy discovered still clutching a rusty sword in its bony grasp. This oak tree subsequently became an object of dread and until it blew down in 1813, local people who had to pass 'the haunted tree' at night would quicken their pace and murmur a prayer to protect them against the evil demon believed to live within it.

When the death penalty was meted out in the past, a nearby oak could be a convenient location for summary justice. For example in 1537, Henry VIII, enraged by the refusal of leading clerics at Woburn Abbey to submit to his will, ordered the whole lot to be hanged from an oak tree in the grounds. The abbot and prior of the abbey, the vicar of Puddington, and 'other contumacious persons' swung from the boughs of the tree, ever-after known as the *Abbot's Oak*. Many of the perpetrators of the Monmouth Rebellion, sentenced to death by the infamous Judge Jeffreys, suffered a similar fate in 1685. Twelve men were despatched on an oak, later dubbed the *Hangcross Tree* at Chard in Somerset. Another six were hanged from the *Heddon Oak* at Crowcombe, which was later said to be haunted. On a quiet night, you could hear the galloping horses bringing the men to execution or the rattling of their chains as they swung from the boughs.

A famous haunted oak once stood in Windsor. *Herne's Oak* was named after a forest keeper who hanged himself from the tree to save himself from being disgraced by some deed that has now long since been forgotten. The man's ghost was said to haunt the tree, shaking chains and spiriting away livestock, and it became famous as a place to avoid at night. Even Shakespeare refers to it in *The Merry Wives of Windsor*:

> Why yet, there want not many that do fear,
> In deep of night to walk by this Herne's Oak.

Oak timber has been an important construction material in Britain for millennia. Stretching back into the Bronze Age, we know that as well as stone circles such as Avebury and Stonehenge, there were wooden ones. So-called 'Seahenge' in Norfolk, for example, was a ring of fifty-five huge oak posts laid out in a circle on marshland. Much of the timber has survived and was from oak trees cut down in 2049 BC. A similar age has been suggested for 'Woodhenge' at Amesbury in Wiltshire.

In later centuries, oak was the favoured material for the important weight-bearing timbers in houses because it was so strong. Oak was the preferred wood for constructing roofs and one of the most famous examples in England is Westminster Hall, part of

The magnificent oak roof of Westminster Hall (left). An oak trunk sawn into lengths will quickly crack if not seasoned properly (top right). The interior of a medieval barn roof, showing the oak timbers used in its construction (below right).

the Houses of Parliament. Its impressive hammer beam construction dates from the fourteenth century and is the biggest medieval timber roof in northern Europe; it is an astonishing 240 feet long and 69 feet wide, and covers around 17,000 square feet. And yet the design of the roof is so sound that not a single supporting column is needed to hold it up, creating a vast unobstructed open space.

Throughout the UK many medieval and Tudor buildings survive, with their oak roofs as a much admired feature, together with flooring, panelling and staircases; many of the characteristic features of church interiors such as pews, decorative screens and pulpits are often made from oak too. Besides all these many uses, oak was, and is, a popular wood from which to make furniture.

Oak was vital to other construction industries too. Shipbuilding has long been associated with the British Isles, and oak was once a vital material in this very old industry. Even our ancient ancestors made boats from oak. The Ferriby boats, for example, are three Bronze Age vessels named after the place in Yorkshire where they were unearthed. One of them may date to as far back as 2000 BC and has been hailed as the oldest seagoing boat in Europe. The construction technique at Ferriby, and in other places where similar boats have been found, was to bind together large planks of oak using young wiry yew branches. However, other boatbuilding methods were also utilised, the simplest being to chop down a large oak tree and hollow the trunk out. Remains of oak logboats from several locations in the UK have been studied. The Hanson logboat from Derbyshire is a Bronze Age vessel, and was made from a 300-year-old oak tree in about 1500 BC. When it sank it was still carrying its cargo of sandstone. The Poole logboat from Dorset is less ancient, but illustrates that similar techniques were still being used over a thousand years later in the Iron Age. It dates to around 300 BC, and was particularly large, seating as many as eighteen people.

In more recent centuries, oak trees became known as 'the fathers of ships'. They were vital to success in the longstanding wars and empire building of the eighteenth and early nineteenth centuries: oak was the first choice for both warships and merchant ships during the era of sail. It could be said that the British Empire was founded on oak. The eighteenth-century poet William Mason wrote:

> *Those sapling oaks which at Britannia's call,*
> *May heave their trunks mature into the main,*
> *And float the bulwarks of her liberty.*

An earlier poem by an anonymous author captures the important connection between the products of the land and the ability to command the seas, and a certain veneration for the oak because it equipped the people of these islands for both peace and war:

HMS *Victory*: launched in 1765, Nelson's flagship at Trafalgar in 1805, and still afloat in 1910. It is now in dry dock. *Victory* has a hull and decks made of oak, which have been repaired and replaced many times since the eighteenth century.

When ships for bloody combat we prepare,
Oak affords plank, and arms our men of war;
Maintains our fires, makes ploughs to till the ground;
For use no timber like the oak is found.
Our fleets, that now the seas command,
Were late upon our island growing;
Her wholesome stores, for every band,
As late within her fields were lowing.

In 1800, the Royal Navy had a vast fleet of ships – around 800 of them – all made from oak and hence the service was often referred to as 'the wooden walls of old England'. Nelson's ship, HMS *Victory*, for example, is made of oak, and one estimate suggests that 5,000 oaks were needed for its construction. Oak was said to be ideal for shipbuilding for it was hard, would support a great weight, resisted strain, rotted slowly, and was less likely than other woods to be splintered by cannon shot. In the eighteenth century, the song *Heart of Oak* became popularly associated with the navy, and has this chorus:

Heart of oak are our ships,
Jolly tars are our men,
We always are ready: steady, boys, steady!
We'll fight and we'll conquer again and again.

The tune of this song is still the one to which the Royal Navy marches on official occasions.

Although timber was the most valuable part of the tree, other elements were important too. For example, oak bark was used to tan leather for centuries. It was an important industry, but in order to stop people felling trees simply to take the bark for tanning, James I issued a law that oaks could only be chopped down for this purpose in April, May or June. Unfortunately, this didn't stop tanners clandestinely stripping bark off living oaks and sometimes sufficiently wounding trees to kill them.

Acorns were an important food source for pigs. Traditionally, swine were fattened on acorns to sustain them through the winter, and pig owners wanted their animals to roam local forests in the autumn to reap this valuable food source. Yet by the thirteenth century this right had been eroded, the monarch refusing pigs access to royal areas such as the New Forest. This was one of the many grievances that the barons took up with King John's son Henry III. As a result, an extension of the Magna Carta, called the Charter of the Forest, was agreed and this stated that:

Every free man shall allow his pigs to feed in the forest. We grant also that every free man can move his pigs through our royal forest freely to allow them to feed in his own woods or anywhere else he wishes. And if the pigs of any free man shall spend one night in our forest he shall not on that account be so prosecuted that he loses anything of his own.

Oak apples or oak galls have attracted a great deal of interest for centuries. No one could understand how the tree that produced acorns could sometimes yield something so significantly different. These small rounded balls are, in fact, a reaction to the presence of the gall wasp larva and effectively they act as a protective cocoon in which the insect can mature to adulthood. They gave rise to a certain amount of superstition. Writing in Elizabethan England, the herbalist John Gerard claimed they could foretell the future:

> The oak apples being broken in sunder about the time of their withering, do foreshow the sequel of the year, as the expert Kentish husbandmen have observed by the living things found in them: as if they find an ant they foretell plenty of grain to ensure; if a white worm like a gentill [= fly larva] or a maggot then they prognosticate murrain [= disease] of beasts and cattle; if a spider then (say they) we shall have a pestilence or some such-like sickness to follow amongst men. These things the learned also have observed and noted.

There are many different versions of this superstition. Often the day on which to officially prognosticate using oak apples was Michaelmas Day (29 September). So-called Oak Apple Day was once a public holiday in the UK on 29 May. It commemorated Charles II being restored to the throne, and its name is derived from the famous scene in which the King evaded capture by hiding in an oak tree.

Oak galls had a much more important and practical application, however. Until the beginning of the twentieth century, most of the world's ink was made using oak galls (and the galls from other trees). The galls were boiled in water and when mixed with

Men beating down acorns to feed their pigs in the woods, from the Queen Mary Psalter created between 1310 and 1320. (*Courtesy of the British Library illuminated manuscripts collection www.bl.uk*)

iron sulphate ('copperas') it yielded ink. There were other ways to make ink, but this was overwhelmingly the preferred product. One popular seventeenth-century recipe was:

> The best ink is made in the following manner: Take of galls four ounces, of copperas two ounces, of gum arabic one ounce; beat the galls to a gross powder, and infuse them nine days in a quart of claret, set it near the fire, and stir it daily; then put in the copperas and the gum, and when it has stood a day the ink will be fit for use.

It was a simple chemical reaction, but it was the basis of a major medium of communication and record-keeping for centuries – letters, newspapers, books, registers, reports and accounts. However, on a lighter note, it enabled a rather mean but well-known practical joke, as one Victorian writer recalled in 1866:

> Before the victim went to wash his hands, some of the decoction of galls was poured into the water, while the towel with which he was supplied had been damped with copperas solution and then dried. The consequence of this combination was that, although the hands and face might be washed perfectly clean, yet, as soon as they were dried with the prepared towel, the union of the two substances produced ink, and both hands and face were deeply stained.

A common feature of the UK countryside, especially in England: an oak in early spring leaf.

Pear

*D*etails from a clay tablet show that the Assyrians were eating pears by the eighteenth century BC, and the ancient Persians are known to have grown them as crops. The common pear tree (*Pyrus communis*) probably originates from western Asia and is not native to the UK. All cultivated European pears sold in shops these days are ultimately varieties of this species.

However, there are many other species of pear. One called the wild pear (*Pyrus pyraster*) grows in hedges, waste ground and woodland margins in the UK, and bears small, round, hard fruit that are not eaten. Various types of small, sharp-tasting pears considered to be 'wild pears' were called 'choke pears' in former times and were sometimes juiced to make drinks or medicines. There are separate species that produce the fruit known as 'Asian pears' or 'Chinese pears'.

It is often assumed that the Romans introduced the common pear tree to their province of Britannia, since they were so fond of the fruit. The tree has been a UK resident for a long time – pear seeds have been found at Anglo-Saxon sites, and pear trees are mentioned as boundary markers in the Domesday Book and in Anglo-Saxon manuscripts.

Even in Roman times, however, many different varieties of pear were known: Pliny recognised forty-one of them in the first century. Here are his descriptions of four varieties:

> A similar degree of precociousness has caused the name 'superbum' ['proud'] to be given to one species of pear: it is a small fruit, but ripens with remarkable speed. All the world are extremely partial to the Crustumian pear; and next to it comes the Falernian, so called from the drink which it affords, so abundant is its juice. This juice is known by the name of 'milk' in the variety which, of a black colour, is by some called the pear of Syria. The names given to other varieties depend upon the respective localities of their growth.

The legendary King Mark of Cornwall hides in a pear tree to spy on his wife with her lover in this thirteenth-century English manuscript. (*Courtesy of the British Library illuminated manuscripts collection www.bl.uk 11619 f. 8*)

For a long time many esteemed varieties of pear were imported from France, but they were also frequently homegrown in the grounds of medieval monasteries in the UK. Some of these pear orchards were very extensive. Warden Abbey in Bedfordshire is credited with creating the first new variety of English pear that was widely enjoyed across the land. The Warden pear was popular and rapidly taken up and cultivated in other areas of the UK, even Scotland. It was a variety that kept well, although like most standard varieties of the period it had to be cooked before eating. Warden pie was a dessert that was relished throughout the country for centuries, and is mentioned by Shakespeare in *The Winter's Tale*: 'I must have saffron to colour the warden pies.' A cookery book from 1591 recommends this recipe:

How to bake Wardens.
Core your wardens and pare them, and perboyle them and laye them in your paste [= pastry], and put in every warden where you take out the core a clove or twain [= two]; put to them sugar, ginger, sinamon – more sinamon then ginger – make your crust very fine and somewhat thick, and bake them leisurely.

In briefly describing pears in England, the Tudor herbalist John Gerard admitted that he would need a whole book to do the subject justice. He goes on to say that one grower of his acquaintance cultivated around sixty different varieties, and that there were many more available. Gerard explains that areas of London now long since given over to offices and housing were in his day famous large-scale pear orchards:

The tame [= cultivated] pear trees are planted in orchards, as be the apple trees, and by grafting upon wild stocks come much variety of good and pleasant fruits. All these [varieties] before specified, and many sorts more, and those most rare and good, are growing in the ground of Master Richard Pointer, a most cunning and curious grafter and planter of all manner of rare fruits, dwelling in a small village near London called Twickenham; and also in the ground of an excellent grafter and painful [= careful] planter, Mr Henry Banbury of Touthill Street(1) near Westminster, and likewise in the ground of a diligent and most affectionate lover of plants, Mr Warner near Horsey Down(2) by London, and in diverse other grounds about London. Most of the best pears are at this day to be had with Mr John Millen in Old Street,(3) in whose nursey are to be found the choicest fruits this kingdom yields.

(1) Touthill Street is modern Tothill Street, opposite the entrance to Westminster Abbey.

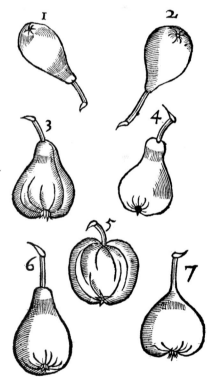

Seven example varieties of pear from Tudor England identified by John Gerrard: 1. Jenneting pear; 2. St James pear; 3. Pear Royal; 4. Burgomot pear; 5. Quince pear; 6. Bishops pear; 7. Winter pear.

(2) Horsey Down or Horselydown was near Tower Bridge, opposite St Katharine Docks.
(3) Old Street is probably the road still bearing the same name in Clerkenwell.

The city of Worcester has long been associated with pears, because large numbers of pear orchards used to grow in the vicinity. It became the heart of the UK's pear cultivation industry, and Worcester's coat of arms still displays pears. When Charles I moved one of the royal mints there during the Civil War, coins were struck that included small pears as mint marks. Worcester has also been a principal site for the production of an alcoholic drink made from pears called perry.

There are many versions of the coat of arms of Worcester but all feature a tower or fortification with three black pears, which can be seen here in the top left-hand corner.

Gerard notes that 'all manner of pears do bind and stop the belly' and that they were good for treating diarrhoea or dysentery. The later herbalist Nicholas Culpeper is slightly at odds with Gerard. He claims that although the hard or sour varieties of pear bind the belly, the 'sweet and luscious' sorts of pears 'help to move the belly downwards' – in other words they act as a mild laxative. This probably reflects an increased availability of 'dessert pears' in England in Culpeper's time: varieties that are sweet and soft and can be eaten raw. Until the nineteenth century, most varieties of pears were cooked before eating.

A widely grown British variety that did not need cooking was the Williams' pear. This cultivar arose by chance. A schoolmaster in Aldermaston named Mr Wheeler found a small pear tree growing in his garden in about 1770. He decided to leave the tree to see if it would bear fruit. The first crops were the beautifully sweet, tender and

---

Fruits of success

Perry may have existed in Roman times. The quote from Pliny at the beginning of this chapter mentions a drink made from the Falernian variety of pear. In the Elizabethan era, Gerard speaks of it with approval:

> Wine made of the juice of pears, called in English perry, is soluble, [and] purges those that are not accustomed to drink thereof, especially when it is new; notwithstanding, it is as wholesome a drink, being taken in small quantity, as wine; it comforteth and warmeth the stomach, and causeth good digestion.

The most famous perry in the UK is a sparkling drink with the brand name Babycham, developed by a brewer named Francis Showering from Shepton Mallet in Somerset. It was launched nationally in the UK in 1953 and was originally aimed at a female clientele. In 1957, Babycham was the subject of the first ever advert for an alcoholic drink on commercial television in the UK.

Pear tree blossom.

Prize-winning pear

The first National Pear Conference was held at Chiswick in 1885, where delegates studied and evaluated over 600 varieties of pear submitted mostly by UK growers. Importantly, the event witnessed the earliest public appearance of a new variety of pear grown by Thomas Francis Rivers from Hertfordshire. It was named in honour of the proceedings – the Conference pear. It is now the most commonly grown pear variety in Europe.

juicy pears for which this variety has become famous. It became extremely popular after being propagated in the nurseries of a London grower, Mr Williams, and this is how it acquired its name. Another popular variety that is still grown is Comice, which was developed in France in the mid-nineteenth century.

It was formerly said that 'He who plants pears, plants for his heirs' because older varieties of pear grown from seed could take a long time to mature sufficiently to produce a commercially valuable crop each year. However, newer varieties in the nineteenth century, propagated by techniques such as grafting, matured quickly and cropped heavily.

John Evelyn notes that the wood of the tree was not to be neglected. He described it thus: 'useful is the pear tree for its excellent coloured timber (seldom or never worm-eaten) especially for stools, tables, chairs, cabinets, and very many works of the joiner and sculptor.' Pear timber was easy to carve and was often used for the woodblocks responsible for the images in manually printed books. A similar process allowed pictures or patterns to be stamped on to textiles.

Woodblock depicting *Ambrosia altera* carved in pear wood with a copy of the sixteenth-century text as printed in Prague in 1562–63. It was designed by Giorgio Liberale and cut by Wolfgang Meyerpeck for Pietro Andrea Mattioli's *Herbár and New Kreuterbeuch*. (*Courtesy of Wellcome Collection https://wellcomecollection.org*)

Pine

Common conifers in the UK include several species of pine, fir, spruce, larch and cedar, which are all members of the pine family (pinaceae). These species provide us with our traditional Christmas tree, with many different cultivars being created specifically for the purpose. The most well-known Christmas tree in the country is a large specimen of Norway spruce donated to London every year by the people of Oslo as a token of gratitude for the UK's assistance in the Second World War. It is cut down in November and brought across the North Sea by ship. The use of decorated conifers in UK households is a firmly established aspect of our Christmas celebrations, but it was a custom copied from Germany relatively recently. Members of the British Royal Family with close family in Germany helped to popularise the idea of the Christmas tree, including George III's wife, Queen Charlotte, and most famously, Queen Victoria's husband, Albert.

Despite the large number of pine family species in the world, the only one actually native to the UK is the Scots pine, which was formerly known as the wild pine or Scots fir. There are two other native conifers that are not pines: the juniper, famous for its berries providing the customary flavouring for gin, and the yew (see separate chapter). In 2014, a public consultation resulted in the Scots pine being elected as the National Tree of Scotland, with 52 per cent of voters choosing it. It is a very fitting choice, since it is the dominant tree species of the Caledonian pinewoods of the Highlands, for which Scotland is so famous.

The Christmas tree given to London by the people of Norway every year.

Unfortunately, many areas of natural pine woodland were decimated in the past. Nineteenth-century Scottish author Thomas Lauder described the trees of the Highlands being 'unmercifully slaughtered'. The interminable wars of the eighteenth and early nineteenth centuries made it hard to import timber, and native trees were targeted instead because wood was such an essential construction commodity. Writing towards the end of the wars with Napoleon, Walter Nicol wrote about the over-zealous felling of Scottish trees:

> Owing to the scarcity, and high price, of foreign timber of late years, the demand for Highland fir has very much increased. Indeed, the high price given has been the cause of much premature felling, and many of the Scots' natural forests are now very much lessened in extent by the operation of these causes.

The pine from the Rothiemurchus area, for example, was once much prized. The tall hardy trees gave wood of excellent quality and were a particularly good source of the resin used to make turpentine or 'turps'. In the early nineteenth century, the trees were still so abundant that they were chopped down in large numbers and the trunks floated down the river Spey en masse like a giant raft.

Felled trunks of pine awaiting transportation.

A Scots pine plantation.

An inscription recorded at Gordon Castle, Moray, describes another example of how Scottish forests were cleared of pine:

In the year 1783, William Osbourne esquire, merchant of Hull, purchased of the Duke of Gordon the forest of Glenmore, the whole of which he cut down in the space of twenty-two years, and built during that time, at the mouth of the river Spey where never vessel was built before, forty-seven sail of ships of upwards of 19,000 tons burthen. The largest of them of 1,050 tons, and three others little inferior in size, are now in the service of His Majesty and the Honourable East India Company. This undertaking was completed at the expense (of labour only) of above £70,000.

Pine has become a valued timber because the trees grow straight and tall, they are easy to cultivate even on poor soil or in exposed areas, they will grow quite densely packed together, and they quickly reach a size where they can be profitably felled. The wood is not difficult to work and it is the 'builder's timber' with innumerable essential housebuilding roles: from roofs to joists to window frames. It is also a wood from which furniture, fences, building pallets and sheds are frequently made. Although pine was occasionally selected for constructing ships' hulls in the UK, it was not a favoured timber because it was not as durable as many alternatives. Yet it was often utilised for this purpose by the Vikings because the tree grows so commonly in Scandinavia, and

Pine in flower.

the Romans used it for shipbuilding too. Even in the UK, where wood such as oak was preferred for building wooden vessels, the masts were generally made from tall, straight pine trunks as well as the spars that crossed them to carry the sails.

Given its value as wood, pine began to be deliberately planted to produce timber at the end of the seventeenth century. In England, for example, the Marquis of Bath created a Scots pine plantation in Wiltshire in 1696, and a century later his manager, Thomas Davis, planted upwards of 25,000 new trees. Plantations sprang up all over the UK, especially in areas of relatively poor soil or where the land could not be put to better use because it was very hilly. The trees were felled every twenty-five to thirty years. Despite this, the UK imported vast quantities of pine during peacetime, especially from the countries bordering the Baltic.

The pine has had a large number of medical uses in the past. The seventeenth-century writer John Evelyn summed up some common properties that he was aware of:

> The bark of the pine heals ulcers; and the inner rind, cut small and boiled in store of water, is an excellent remedy for burns and scalds, washing the sore with the decoction and applying the softened bark. It is also sovereign against frozen and benumbed limbs. The distilled water of the green cones takes away the wrinkles of the face, dipping cloths therein and laying them on, it becomes a cosmetic not to be despised.

Additional medical uses are recorded by John Pechey:

> The bark and leaves cool and bind; wherefore they are good in dysenteries, and fluxes of the courses [= heavy menstruations]. A decoction or infusion of the tops in beer, or some other proper liquor, is reckon'd very good for the stone of the kidneys and bladder, and for the scurvy, and diseases of the breast. The nuts have a delicate taste, and are good for coughs and consumptions, and for heat of urine [= cystitis]. They increase milk, and provoke venery [= lust].

Ancient reverence

The pine tree was sacred to the Greeks and Romans in many different ways. In one tradition, the goddess Cybele transformed her lover Attis into a pine tree to save him from self-destruction; in another tale, one of Pan's lovers was transformed into a pine to escape unwelcome attentions. Hence the pine is connected with both deities.

But it doesn't end there. The pine was associated with Bacchus, the god of wine, and his spear was always topped with a pine cone; as a result, Greeks put pine cones into their wine to help preserve it. Finally, the tree was additionally consecrated to Neptune, god of the sea, because early ships were commonly made from pine. Victors at the Isthmian games, held every other year in honour of Neptune, received a garland of pine leaves.

As a result of these multiple connections, pine cones and pine trees were frequently incorporated into Greek and Roman art and design.

Sunrise over Scots pine forest.

Poplar

Black poplar.

*T*here are many species of poplar; the name comes from Norman French and the term seems to have been brought into English after William the Conqueror's victory at Hastings.

The black poplar (*Populus nigra*) is a native tree that was once very common in England and Wales. The London area known as Poplar is so called because it was once a hamlet near the Thames where there was an abundance of poplar trees, many of which were still standing in the eighteenth century. Poplars feature prominently in John Constable's painting *The Hay Wain*. This portrays a countryside landscape on the river Stour in south-east England with lofty poplar trees, in front of which a horse-drawn cart and driver have paused in the water. Poplar timber was used for building farm vehicles, so the cart in Constable's picture may actually be built from its wood. The riverside setting for the scene is also apt: the black poplar was widely known as the water poplar because it tends to grow in wet conditions. In parts of eastern England it was called the cotton tree because of the fluffy white seeds produced by female trees.

Since the time when Constable painted his picture in 1821, the black poplar has become a rare native tree. It is not the most elegant of trees so is not often planted by choice, and both the drainage of land and clearance of floodplains has robbed it of its preferred growing conditions. There are now only a few thousand left.

Poplars tend to grow in clusters, and there is a charming mythology that seeks to explain this observation. The Greek sun god Helios had a son called Phaethon who

White poplar leaves on a windy day, showing their characteristic white undersides.

demanded to be allowed to drive the chariot that drew the sun across the sky. He was permitted to do so, but lost control of the horses. Zeus, alarmed that the sun would burn the Earth, struck the chariot down with a lightning bolt, which saved the world, but killed the unruly Phaethon who was thrown into the river Po. His sisters were so distraught that they gathered together, wandering the riverside searching for him, and wouldn't stop crying. Out of sympathy (or maybe exasperation with the family), Zeus turned the tearful women into a cluster of poplar trees. This allusion was perhaps further fuelled by the fact that poplar trees can drip sticky moisture during the summer, which might be said to resemble tears.

Drawing of Hercules with his poplar wreath from about 1792. (*Courtesy of Wellcome Collection https://wellcomecollection.org*)

Another species, the white poplar (*Populus alba*), is nowadays much more common than the black poplar although it is not a native tree. It is, however, a longstanding resident of the UK and was formerly widely known by a Norman term, the *abele*. The white poplar derives its name from the fact that the tree's green leaves are very pale on the underside. On a blustery day the leaves are blown backwards, giving the impression that the tree has suddenly changed colour.

The white poplar had important mythological connections in ancient times. Leuce (meaning 'white') was a beautiful daughter of the sea deity, Oceanus. The god of the underworld, Pluto, fell hopelessly in love with her and in desperation, he abducted her. Leuce lived her mortal life with Pluto, and when she died the god created a new tree to honour her memory: the white poplar. The same tree was consecrated to the hero Hercules as well. This is because he fought a fire-breathing giant named Cacus in a cavern near the Aventine Hill, which was covered with these trees. When Hercules emerged triumphant from the fight, he grabbed a branch of white poplar and tied it around his head like a victory wreath. The hot sweat from the hero's forehead blanched the undersides of the leaves and made them the white colour that they are today. Those who made sacrifices to Hercules or who commemorated his memory always wore a white poplar wreath.

Robin Hood in action – the shafts of arrows were often made from poplar wood because it was lightweight and easy to cut.

Poplars had a range of medicinal uses in the past. Since ancient times the bark of the poplar was a treatment for sciatica. The Roman writer Sammonicus related a little rhyme attesting the tree's powers:

> *A hidden disease doth oft rage and reign:*
> *The hip overcome, and vex with pain.*
> *It makes with vile aching: one treads slow and do shrink,*
> *The bark of white polar is help in drink.*

Sixteenth-century herbalist John Gerard explained that poplar can take away women's fertility, and the 'warme juice of the leaves being dropped into the eares doth take away the paine thereof'. He reports that an ointment made from poplar buds was given various names including popilion, pompillion, and *unguentum populeon*. This was well known to the apothecaries and was 'good against all inflammations, bruses, squats,

---

Shiver me timbers

One native species of poplar was formerly called the trembling poplar because its leaves seemed particularly inclined to shiver, even at the lightest breeze. It is now more familiarly known to us as the aspen (*Populus tremula*) and by various means it was accounted a cure for 'the shakes' in humans known as the ague. The herbalist John Gerard reported, rather cheekily, that the constantly moving leaves must be made of the same matter as women's tongues since both seldom ceased wagging.

Christian writers believed that aspen leaves quaked out of shame and horror from the recollection that Christ's cross was allegedly made of its timber. The leaves were said to be struggling to escape the wicked wood on which they grew; the only time they were ever supposed to be still was Christmas night.

Tennyson describes this well-known tremulous feature of the aspen in *The Lady of Shalott*:

> *Willows whiten, aspens quiver,*
> *Little breezes dusk and shiver*

Victorian illustration of aspen.

A traditional English proverb 'to tremble like an aspen leaf' described people who were fearful or anxious, and poets have widely used the same metaphor. In John Keats' *Endymion*, the poem's central character is portrayed as 'trembling like an aspen-bough' and in *Titus Andronicus*, Shakespeare describes Philomela's lily-white hands that 'tremble, like aspen leaves, upon a lute'.

falls, and such like'. Nicholas Culpeper asserted that the ointment dried up the milk of women's breasts when they had weaned their children. Amongst other medicinal uses, Culpeper says that poplar leaves bruised and soaked in vinegar were applied to joints to ease gout, and that the seeds added to vinegar were valuable to treat 'the falling sickness' (epilepsy). John Evelyn described an eyewash made from poplar buds and honey that was recommended during his time to induce sleep, and John Pechey revealed that 'women use the buds of black poplar to beautifie and thicken their hair'.

Poplar timber of all kinds is relatively soft and not very durable, but it is light in weight and easy to work. Hence, it was a cheap option for making everyday items like short-lived farmyard equipment, wooden toys, building frames, trays, bowls, clothes pegs, animal feeding troughs, floorboards for agricultural buildings, and packing cases for transporting goods. Although a variety of woods were available to make the shafts of arrows, analysis of those found in the wreck of the Tudor warship *Mary Rose* show that poplar comprises over three-quarters of them. In some parts of the UK, poplar wood was preferred for fitting out a dairy because it was believed that mice did not like it and so would not enter.

The wood is not very flammable so it burns slowly, which made it popular as a fuel for ovens where a constant steady heat was required; it has also been used to make matches, and in more recent times to line the interiors of saunas.

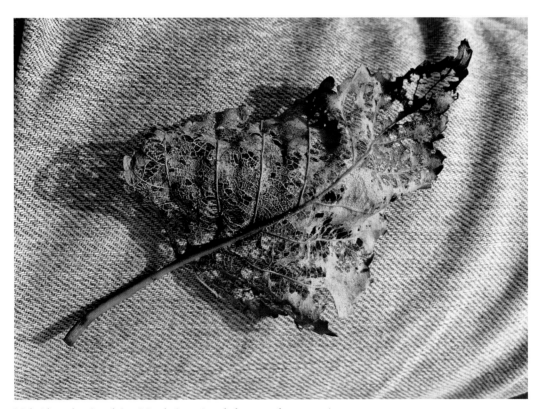

Hybrid poplars involving North American balsam poplars are quite common.

A whole variety of poplar hybrids have arisen. A longstanding stable one that has existed for centuries is the grey poplar, which is a cross between a white poplar and an aspen. However, in more modern times the number of hybrids and cultivars created artificially has increased considerably, such that they can be quite difficult to identify. Some of them involve balsam poplars as one of the parent plants – this group of poplars is indigenous to North America and parts of Asia and their buds have a distinctive aromatic scent.

However, perhaps the most famous cultivar is the Lombardy poplar, which, as its named suggests, originates from Italy. It is a cultivar of the black poplar known as 'Italica', and was introduced to Britain in the mid-eighteenth century. The tree is remarkably tall and narrow with very short side branches and quickly became very fashionable. Yet by 1810, garden designer Walter Nicol admitted that he did not like them:

Excepting near the cathedral at Dunkeld in Perthshire, we do not recollect of having seen a Lombardy poplar that could be looked upon with any degree of pleasure. We think it a very ugly tree… The prevalence of poplars in the vicinity of London, and other places in England, is tiresome in the extreme.

A line of Lombardy poplars.

In the 1830s, garden designer John Claudius Loudon also railed against the inappropriate use of Lombardy poplars in suburban gardens near to houses, and in destroying the harmony of larger estates when sited without careful planning. These trees could look beautiful if planted by a skilled designer (such as, perhaps, himself), but so often other people failed. The Lombardy poplar was, he concluded, 'a most dangerous tree in the hands of a planter who has not considerable knowledge and good taste in the composition of landscape'. However, he noted that it was a tree that could do well in an urban setting:

> The suitableness of the Lombardy poplar for planting in towns and cities arises not only from its narrow form and vertical direction, but also from its nature; which… admits of its thriving even among coal smoke, where most other trees would die or become stunted and diseased.

Nonetheless, the Lombardy poplar remains a commonly planted tree in the UK – often in long lines, marching along like a column of soldiers.

Rowan

The characteristic pinnate
leaves of rowan with their
serrated margins.

*T*his tree has had a wide variety of alternative names, the most common being 'mountain ash', which rivals the name rowan in terms of modern popularity. Other titles have included quickbeam, ornus, wild sorb, flowering ash, water elder, quicken tree, wild ash, whitten tree, wiggan and witchen. The name 'quickbeam' is known from Anglo Saxon times, with quick meaning 'alive' as in the once-familiar phrase 'the quick and the dead' from the King James version of the Bible. The word 'beam' was Old English for tree, so the quickbeam was the tree that was alive or the 'tree of vitality'. How the rowan acquired this unusual name is unclear, but the springy nature of the tree's young branches and its multiple small leaves give it a certain animation that may have inspired the title. The tree also has a longstanding reputation for being protective against the supernatural, so 'quick' may perhaps imply an ability to continue to live or to survive despite the forces of evil.

Rowan tree blossom.

William Turner noted in his herbal of 1562 that there were distinct preferences for this tree's name, depending on where in the UK a person came from: 'The tree which we call in the north country a quicken tree or a rowan tree, and in the south country a quickbeam.' The name rowan was originally confined mostly to Scotland and is of Norse origin. Interestingly, a folklore tale from the north of Britain made a direct connection with the old Norse gods. Here, the rowan was known as 'Thor's Helper' because when trying to evade the clutches of an evil sorceress, the great god only managed to cross a swollen river and escape by grabbing hold of some rowan trees to haul himself out of danger.

Since Thor was the God of Thunder, it was only natural that he would avoid striking anyone who took shelter by one of these trees. Rowan was one of a number of plants said to offer protection from lightning. We will never know for certain why these few species were singled out, but it might have been inspired by their physical features. The serrated pinnate leaves of rowan, for example, may have put our ancestors in mind of the jagged shape of lightning in the sky, and its orange-red berries were potentially a reminder of the fire and heat that a lightning strike can generate.

Rowan berries were brewed to make beer in Wales; in Scotland and England they were used to make jam.

The rowan's defence against the forces of darkness took many forms. For example, there was a tradition in some parts of the country, especially the north, that including a small amount of rowan wood within the construction of a ship would protect it from harm. If the churning of milk failed to produce butter then it had been cursed by a witch, and a rowan stirring stick might reverse the spell. Similarly, the stock of a whip used to drive horses ought to be made of rowan to stop the horses becoming bewitched and bolting. This custom was embodied in an old adage:

> *If your whipsticks made of row'n,*
> *You may ride your nag through any town.*

The seventeenth-century diarist John Evelyn described the particular respect with which the rowan was held in Wales during his time:

> Ale and beer brewed with these berries, being ripe, is an incomparable drink, familiar in Wales, where this tree is reputed so sacred that there is not a churchyard without one of them planted in it (as among us the yew); so, on a certain day in the year everybody religiously wears a cross made of the wood; and the tree is by some authors called Fraxinus Cambro-Britannica ['Welsh-British ash'], reputed to be a preservative against fascinations and evil spirits; whence, perhaps, we call it witchen, the boughs being stuck about the house or the wood used for walking-staves.

The rowan's ability to actually dispel witchcraft was recorded in the seventeenth century. William Williams, in his *Occult Physick* (1660), describes the effects of the tree:

> Take a cluster of quick-bane tree berries green, and convey them about the party suspected to be a witch, and then examine her and she shall confess. Pound the same berries and strain them and give them to any beast or man that is overseen by a witch or witchcraft, and it helpeth them.

Witches' powers were inhibited by the rowan tree – a branch thrown in her path would stop her in her tracks, or even send her packing, hence John Evelyn's note about the popularity of the tree for walking sticks. Who knows when you might come across a malevolent witch

The rowan was a valuable agent against witches. (*Courtesy of Wellcome Collection https://wellcomecollection.org*).

when out for stroll? In some parts of England, it was common to plant rowan trees near the front door or to have branches of it in the house to ward away witches. In 1866, William Henderson collected together many superstitions from the north of Britain and includes this tale as related to him by a local clergyman:

> The other day I cut down a mountain ash (or wiggan tree as it is called here) in my carriage road. The old man who gardens for me came a day or two after, and was strangely disconcerted on seeing what 'master' had done in his absence; 'for' said he, 'wherever a wiggan tree grows near a house, the witches canna come.' He was comforted, however, by finding, on closer investigation, that a sucker from the tree had escaped destruction.

Witches were prone to entering houses by the chimney so rowan was often displayed above the fireplace to stop them coming in. In Wales and Scotland, even in Victorian times, a rowan branch might be chosen to drive cattle to prevent their becoming bewitched, and branches were hung up over doorways and cowsheds for similar reasons. A popular rhyme in Scotland advised combining the protective powers of rowan with red thread, another agent believed to guard against evil forces:

> *Rowan tree and red thread,*
> *Put the witches to their speed.*

A rowan tree cross bound with red thread was seen as an especially powerful form of apotropaism – the use of magic or a charm to defend against the influence of evil and the supernatural. Some people carried a stick of the tree around with them or gave it to their children when away from home. William Henderson has another interesting Victorian anecdote about this practice:

> A woman was lately in my shop, and in pulling out her purse brought out also a piece of stick a few inches long. I asked her why she carried that in her pocket. 'Oh,' she replied, 'I must not lose that, or I shall be done for.'
> 'Why so?' I inquired.
> 'Well,' she answered, 'I carry that to keep off the witches; while I have that about me, they cannot hurt me.' On my adding that there were no witches nowadays, she instantly replied, 'Oh, yes! there are thirteen at this very time in the town, but so long as I have my rowan-tree safe in my pocket they cannot hurt me.'

Folklorist Charles Leland noted having seen this practice in a book published as late as 1891. He observed a twig of rowan tree 'wound round with some dozens of yards of red thread, placed visible in the window to act as a charm in keeping witches and boggle-boes from the house'.

A charm against the forces of evil – rowan twigs bound with red thread.

Despite its supposedly magical properties, the rowan was given surprisingly limited attention as a medicine. Thomas Elliott, in his *Castell of Healthe*, published about 1537, stated that quickbeam was a potential treatment for depression or a 'purger of melancholy' as he poetically called it. In the seventeenth century, rowan berries were cited as a treatment for scurvy and disorders of the spleen.

However, rowan wood did find some practical uses. It was used to make handles for tools and ploughs, for poles, and was noted as a good second choice wood for longbows if yew was unavailable. Rowan trees were grown on estates for their decorative flowers and berries, but the speed of the trees' growth made them good 'nurses' for slower growing trees – protecting them from bad weather until they were strong enough to survive undefended.

Sweet Chestnut

Looking up in a
forest of coppiced
sweet chestnut.

*T*he sweet chestnut is not native to the UK, and it is generally supposed that the tree was introduced by the Romans. Indeed, the word 'chestnut' is ultimately derived from its Latin name *castanea*. The Roman writer Pliny identifies eighteen different varieties of chestnut known to him in the first century. It is difficult to determine if these were simply natural variations induced by factors such as climate and growing conditions, or whether different varieties had actually been cultivated or encouraged. He goes on to say:

> The chestnut has its armour of defence in a shell bristling with prickles like the hedge-hog, an envelope which in the acorn is only partially developed. It is really surprising, however, that Nature should have taken such pains thus to conceal an object of so little value… Chestnuts are the most pleasant eating when roasted; they are sometimes ground also, and are eaten by women when fasting for religious reasons, as bearing some resemblance to bread.

In the UK, the name 'sweet chestnut' was adopted to distinguish it from the bitter-tasting horse chestnut – both trees producing nuts of similar size and colour, although they are not closely related. The Greeks and Romans had many stories about the origin of the sweet chestnut. Several ancient authors suggest it originally came from the area of modern-day Turkey, and may have been named by the Greeks after a city called Kastana, around which many chestnut trees grew.

The 'Chestnut of a Hundred Horses' (*Castagno dei Cento Cavalli*) in about 1873.

A tree believed to be both the largest and the oldest sweet chestnut in the world can be found on the slopes of Mount Etna in Sicily. It is known as the 'Chestnut of a Hundred Horses' (*Castagno dei Cento Cavalli*) because a queen and her one hundred knights are reputed to have once sheltered beneath its capacious canopy during a storm. It's precise age is not known but has been estmated at over 2,000 years, and although the tree has multiple trunks they are believed to share the same roots. The oldest sweet chestnut in the UK is said to be the large specimen at Tortworth in Gloucestershire, which may be over a thousand years old.

Apart from Italy and the Romans, the sweet chestnut has associations with other European countries. In the UK, the tree was formerly called the Spanish chestnut because particularly tasty chestnuts were imported from Spain. Chestnuts were much valued in France, where many different tree varieties were said to exist in the early nineteenth century, bred to produce especially large and sweet nuts called *marrons*. In some parts of southern Europe, including France and Italy, chestnuts were cooked and converted into a kind of flour for making cakes, puddings and even a form of bread. It is an old custom – as already noted, the Roman writer Pliny mentions it – and the use of chestnut flour for baking continues to this day in places such as Corsica, for example. One anonymous author in 1612 even described the practice in England too: the tree producing 'good fruit that poor people in time of dearth may, with a small quantity of oats or barely, make bread of'.

Freshly gathered chestnuts.

Chestnuts were considered a tasty treat in countries such as France, Italy and Spain, where they were widely eaten. Preparation could involve cooking in a variety of different ways – baking, roasting, smoking, frying, boiling – and a whole host of different flavourings could be added including wines, spices, herbs, salt, rose water, lemon juice, even cheese. Yet chestnuts have not been a common food in the UK. The early nineteenth-century botanist John Claudius Loudon remarked on this:

> Chestnuts are comparatively little used as food in England, as they are seldom eaten except roasted at dessert. They are, however, sometimes stewed with cream and made into a soup, either with milk or gravy. They are also occasionally used as stuffing for fowls and turkey; or stewed and brought to table with salt fish.

Two centuries earlier, John Evelyn was even more dismissive of chestnuts as food:

> We give that fruit to our swine in England, which is amongst the delicacies of princes in other countries… doubtless we might propagate their use amongst our common people, being a food so cheap and so lasting.

So the chestnuts prized by continental noblemen were considered fit only for pigs and paupers in England. However, in the UK, chestnuts do not generally grow to the same size as those from southern Europe and are not as sweet, and this may explain matters. Despite this, the county of Devon was once particularly renowned for its good chestnuts

Chestnuts in their cases or husks.

and some of these were transported to London markets where they were often sold on the streets simply roasted and without any of the elaborate preparative techniques practised on the continent. In the seventeenth century, John Pechey explained that there was a reliable way to determine if a chestnut was fit to eat: 'The good nuts are known from the bad, by putting them in water; for, if they are sound and good they sink, but if otherwise they swim.'

Eating roast chestnuts is a reasonably longstanding practice in the UK, but it seems to have been approached as a seasonal novelty rather than with the enthusiasm that chestnuts were welcomed elsewhere in Europe. Seventeenth-century poet Robert Herrick writes of 'fired chestnuts' that 'leap for joy' as their cases burst, and in describing a hearth, John Milton states that 'blackening chestnuts start and crackle there'.

Chestnuts are said to be best harvested just before they fall from the tree.

John Evelyn goes on to describe that eating raw chestnuts was not considered healthy and might be harmful:

> It is found that the eating of them raw, or in bread (as they do much about Limosin [France]) is apt to swell the belly, though without any other inconvenience that I can learn, and yet some condemn them as dangerous for such as are subject to the gravel in the kidneys [kidney stones], and however cooked and prepared [they are] flatulent, offensive to the head and stomach, and those who are subject to the colic.

Predictably, the chestnut tree and its fruit was believed to have a number of medicinal properties in the past. Nicholas Culpeper describes these folklore uses with his habitual easy-going charm:

CHESNUT TREE
It were as needless to describe a tree so commonly known, as to tell a man he hath gotten a mouth; therefore take the government and virtues of them thus:

> The tree is abundantly under the dominion of Jupiter, and therefore the fruit must needs breed good blood, and yield commendable nourishment to the

body; yet if eaten over-much, they make the blood thick, procure head-ach, and bind the body; the inner skin, that covereth the nut, is of so binding a quality, that a scruple of it taken by a man, or ten grains by a child, soon stops any flux [= diarrhoea] whatsoever. The whole nut being dried and beaten into powder, and a dram taken at a time, is a good remedy to stop the terms [= menstrual periods] in women. If you dry chestnuts, (only the kernels I mean) both the barks being taken away, beat them into powder, and make the powder into an electuary with honey, so have you an admirable remedy for the cough and spitting of blood.

Sweet chestnut, sweet dreams

Like beech leaves, sweet chestnut leaves were sometimes chosen to stuff mattresses. The crackling, rustling noise made by the leaves as you turned over in the night was not unpleasant but something a sleeper had to get used to. In France, such mattresses were called *lits de parlement* or 'talking beds'.

Although chestnut wood is not commonly seen today in the construction industry, in the past it was considered of potential value on account of its hardness and durability. It was sometimes selected alongside oak to construct houses – particularly for roofing – and to manufacture furniture, beds, and the hardwearing elements of mills. In situations where it might be exposed to the elements, such as fence posts and piles, it was at times advocated as superior to oak because it was considered less inclined to rot.

However, a certain amount of caution is necessary when reading old texts referring to the use of chestnut wood in the construction industry. Claims about its historical utility have sometimes arisen because of its similar appearance to certain types of oak such as the timber of the sessile oak (*Quercus petraea*). The eighteenth-century naturalist Gilbert White was one of many who wrote about this potential confusion between chestnut and oak, and also the variable quality of chestnut timber even within the same tree:

> The timber and bark of these trees are so very like oak, as might easily deceive an indifferent observer, but the wood is very shaky, and towards the heart '*cup-shaky*' (that is to say, apt to separate in round pieces like cups), so that the inward parts are of no use. They are bought for the purpose of cooperage, but must make but ordinary barrels, buckets, &c. Chestnut sells for half the

The toothed leaves of the sweet chestnut.

price of oak; but has sometimes been sent into the king's docks, and passed off instead of oak.

Nonetheless, chestnut trees have been frequently coppiced to produce wood used for a variety of functions, including stakes, poles, gates, posts, stiles, fencing, piles and casks. Young chestnut wood was widely held to be far superior in every respect to the wood of older trees for it was stronger and less inclined to splinter. Old trees were rated suitable only as fuel, and were not very good even for this because the wood was inclined to spit a lot during burning. Coppiced chestnut wood was employed for charcoal production, although not being of the finest grade it was unsuited to the production of gunpowder. However, chestnut wood charcoal did find use as a fuel for blacksmiths' forges, for example.

This ancient sweet chestnut in Hampshire is a living titan with a girth of around 6½ metres. It was coppiced in its younger days, and probably began growing from a chestnut that germinated in the 1600s.

Sycamore

Urban tree in fog.

*A*t least partly because it is not a native to the UK, no other tree seems to have attracted such a muddle with respect to its identity as the sycamore (*Acer pseudoplatanus*). The tree we now call the sycamore was in earlier centuries confused with a species of fig tree from the Middle East, probably on account of a crudely similar leaf shape. Indeed, it was even erroneously known in England as the wild fig tree. The botanist John Claudius Loudon explains the nature of the misunderstanding:

> The sycamore in the language of flowers signifies curiosity, because it was supposed to be the tree on which Zaccheus climbed to see Christ pass on his way to Jerusalem, when the people strewed leaves and branches of palm and other trees in his way, exclaiming 'Hosanna to the Son of David!' The tree called the sycamore in the Bible, however, was not the *Acer pseudoplatanus*, but the *Ficus sycomorus*, though the supposition that the first was the sycamore of the Scriptures induced many religious persons in the fourteenth and fifteenth centuries to plant it near their houses and in their gardens.

The sycamore is actually a member of the group of trees called maples, which botanically are known as the *Acer* genus. However, the confusion surrounding the naming and identity of this tree does not end there. Its scientific name *Acer pseudoplatanus* means 'the maple that looks like a plane tree' since the leaves do have some resemblance to

Sycamore's scientific name means 'resembling the plane tree' because the leaves are similar; a plane tree leaf is shown on the left and a sycamore on the right.

those of a plane tree, and other names for it in the past were the false plane tree or the mock-plane. As Nicholas Culpeper remarked, 'Those trees vulgarly called sycamores in England, are maples'; many educated people did understand this, and its commonest name in the UK before the universal adoption of 'sycamore' was in fact the great maple.

The word 'sycamore' is derived from Norman French, appropriately enough since the tree came to the UK originally from continental Europe probably in the fifteenth or sixteenth century. In the US it is known more accurately as the sycamore maple. The sycamore is a tree particularly associated with Scotland, where it grows well, and further alternative names in the past, to add to the lengthy list, include the Scottish maple and the Celtic maple. The writer Sir Thomas Lauder offered an explanation for this apparently longstanding connection between his nation and the sycamore: 'It is a favourite Scotch tree, having been much planted about old aristocratic residences in Scotland... it is probable that the long intimacy which subsisted between France and Scotland may be the cause of its being so prevalent in the latter country.'

More sinisterly, sycamore trees were associated with executions in some parts of Scotland. Dule trees or grief trees were used as places to hang people by Scottish barons until perhaps as late as the eighteenth century. These trees had to be tall and sturdy, and sycamores were ideally suited to the task. Often they were selected because they grew

The double-winged seeds of sycamore are often called 'helicopters' by children in the UK because they spin as they fall to the ground.

near a nobleman's residence, making it easier to ensure that a villain would be despatched speedily after sentencing. Perhaps the most famous example of such a tree once grew at Cassilis Castle in Ayrshire, where John Faa, king of the gypsies, was reputedly hanged for attempting to run away with the Countess of Cassilis in the sixteenth century. There are sycamore trees still standing in Scotland that are said to have been dule trees. One example is at Leith Hall, Aberdeenshire, and another at Blairquhan Castle, South Ayrshire.

Tudor herbalist John Gerard gives a fine description of the sycamore:

The great maple is a beautiful and high tree, with a bark of a mean smoothness; the substance of the wood is tender and easy to work on. It sendeth forth on every side very many goodly boughs and branches, which make an excellent shadow against the heat of the sun, upon which are great, broad, and cornered leaves, much like to those of the vine, hanging by long reddish stalks. The flowers hang by clusters of whitish green colour; after them cometh up long fruit fastened together by couples, one right against the other, with kernels bumping out near to the place in which they are combined: in all other parts, flat and thin like unto parchment, or resembling the innermost wings of grasshoppers. The kernels be white and little.

However, even in the seventeenth century it was not as common as it is today. The herbalist John Parkinson wrote in 1640: 'It is nowhere found wild or natural in our land that I can learn, but only planted in orchards or walks for the shadow's sake.' When chosen by landowners, the sycamore's virtues were that it was tall, elegant, fast-growing, and provided a good windbreak. It was used to create avenues, screens and shady sheltered walks on country estates. Shade was highly valued in former times when it was unthinkable for 'persons of quality' to expose their bare skin in hot summers or to get a tan. Hence, the especially large leaves of sycamore were welcomed. In *Love's Labour's Lost*, Shakespeare writes:

Under the cool shade of a sycamore
I thought to close mine eyes some half an hour

The large leaves gave rise to a curious scam. In the seventeenth century, the use of dried sycamore and other leaves to adulterate tobacco imported from British plantations in America was so prevalent that George I's parliament had to legislate to outlaw it.

Sycamore was known as a profitable tree because it grew so quickly even in poor soil and could be felled for timber at a younger age than many other large trees. It is especially tolerant of the pollutions found in urban environments and is frequently found by roadsides and in inner-city parks; it will tolerate blasts of salty wind from the sea too. Sycamore was easy to plant, and cheap. In London nurseries in 1838 you could buy 1,000 seedlings for ten shillings, and 6-foot saplings were two shillings each. Not

Newly emerged sycamore leaves in spring.

everyone liked sycamores, however. Writer John Evelyn would have chopped the whole lot down:

> the honey-dew leaves, which fall early (like those of the ash), turn to mucilage and noxious insects, and putrify with the first moisture of the season; so as they contaminate and mar our walks; and are therefore by my consent to be banished from all curious gardens and avenues.

Sycamore produces thousands of winged seeds and eventually, of course, so many trees were planted on estates that large numbers began growing in the countryside; consequently it is now a common naturalised woodland tree throughout the UK. Being a maple, the sycamore has many similar uses as far as its timber is concerned, although in the UK the uses of the wood have historically been rather limited compared to France and Germany, where there has been a longer habit of working it. The sap of the sycamore, like all maples, is sweet and can be tapped, something that, according to Loudon, made the tree popular with children:

Sycamore Gap showing the now famous 'Robin Hood' tree at Hadrian's Wall.

In Scotland, children amuse themselves by cutting openings in the bark, and sipping the sap that flows from its wounds... In England, children suck the wings of the growing keys for the sake of obtaining the sweet exudation that is upon them.

Sycamore sap was also harvested for the domestic manufacture of alcoholic drinks: it was brewed to yield ales in England and fermented to make wine in Scotland.

Apart from the dule tree sycamores in Scotland, there have been a number of other famous specimens in the UK. The Corstorphine Sycamore, growing near Edinburgh, was reputedly the oldest example in the UK when it was toppled by a storm in 1998. Local tradition says it was planted in the fifteenth century, although historians believe that a sixteenth-century origin is more likely. Another ancient Scottish specimen was the Newbattle Abbey Sycamore, Dalkeith, which was planted by order of the Earl of Lothian in 1560, but this too was felled by high winds in 2006. Of trees still standing, maybe the most famous is the Tolpuddle Martyrs' Tree in Dorset. Beneath this tree is the spot where a group of agricultural labourers met in 1834 to form the first trade union. Their action was declared illegal and they were transported to Australia, but later reprieved. Analysis suggests this sycamore was planted in the 1680s. A much younger tree has become famous for nestling perfectly in a big dip in Hadrian's Wall known as Sycamore Gap. It is sometimes known as the Robin Hood Tree because it featured prominently in a scene from the 1991 film *Robin Hood: Prince of Thieves*.

Etching of sycamore by the American artist Ernest Haskell; in the US it is known as the sycamore maple. (*Public domain image courtesy of Metropolitan Museum of Art, New York, www.metmuseum.org*)

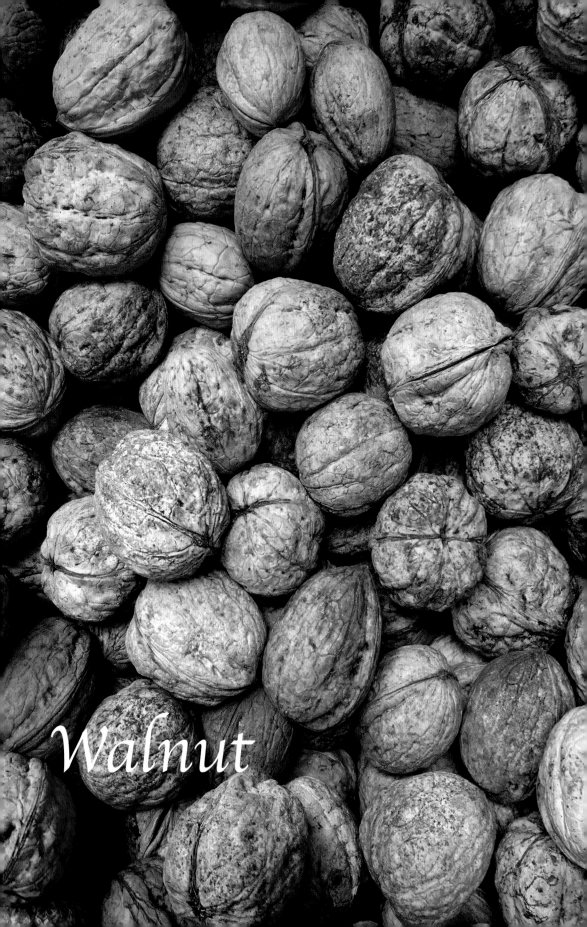

Walnut

*T*he walnut tree is not native to the UK, and it is often assumed that it was introduced by the Romans who held it in high regard. Indeed, the Latin name for the tree is *Juglans regia*, which can be translated as Jupiter's acorn of royalty. The English name walnut can be traced back to Anglo-Saxon roots and is thought to mean 'foreign nut' – a term probably adopted to distinguish it from the more familiar and much more widely available native hazelnut.

According to legend, the walnut tree was introduced into Europe – or at least to the ancient Greeks – by Alexander the Great, who discovered cultivated versions of the tree in Persia. By the time of the Roman Empire, walnut trees were being widely grown to produce the nuts that both Greeks and Romans threw at weddings: the two fused halves of the nut symbolising union and hence fertility. The walnut tree was sacred to Diana the goddess of hunting, the moon, and of women and childbirth.

Walnuts were quite popular ingredients of medieval meals in England. They were added whole to various meat dishes, and ground down to make sauces. Walnuts were also a foodstuff that was allowed to be eaten during the Christian fasting period at Lent. One source records the almoner at Peterborough Abbey buying 1,000 walnuts for his convent at Lent in the mid-fifteenth century.

In the eighteenth and nineteenth centuries, ripe walnuts are often referred to as being a 'dessert fruit', eaten after a meal with wine. However, the unripe nuts – whole with their green husks or just the kernels – were pickled to eat as an accompaniment to main courses.

Walnuts were thought to have medicinal properties too. An enduring theme is the supposed ability of walnuts to counteract poison. Tudor herbalist John Gerard explains:

> Dry nuts taken fasting with a fig and a little rue [herb] withstand poison, prevent and preserve the body from the infection of the plague, and being plentifully eaten they drive worms forth of the belly… With onions, salt and honey they are good against the biting of a mad dog or man, if they be laid upon the wound.

However, it was believed that eating dried walnuts by themselves could be bad for you – causing headaches and chest problems.

The oil expressed from walnuts has been seldom produced in the UK, but was commonly used throughout Europe as wood polish, cooking oil, lamp oil, for making soap, washing the hair, and even for diluting artists' paints. It was popular for making a gentle lotion to soften the skin and to treat bruises, boils, and even hair loss. John Parkinson recommended it in 1629 as 'of excellent use for the coldness, hardness and contracting of the sinews and joints, to warm, supple, and to extend them'.

Walnuts were traditionally collected from trees by beating the ends of branches with long poles, which knocked down the nuts but often broke off the ends of twigs as well, encouraging production of new nut-bearing spurs the next year. This led to a nasty rhyme, which was once often quoted, and probably originated in the sixteenth century: *A woman, a dog, and a walnut tree; The more you beat them, the better they be.*

Maturing walnut tree.

Unripe walnut fruits.

The husks of the fruits were found to produce a dark brown dye that was employed to stain fabric and even human hair in Roman times. It was occasionally used to make ink in the past, and carpenters found it helpful for dyeing light-coloured woods.

The leaves of the tree can give out a strong aromatic smell in hot weather or when crushed, and people believed that this could induce drowsiness or nausea. When macerated into warm water the leaves or the green husks of the fruit made a bitter liquid that found favour for destroying and repelling insects. In the seventeenth century, the same liquid was said to kill worms in lawns, paths and bowling greens, where it 'does infallibly kill the worms without endangering the grass'.

Walnut wood was highly prized, and before the widescale introduction of mahogany it was seen as the most prestigious timber with which to make fine quality furniture. Walnut wood is easy to work, durable, and contains beautiful patterns; it is more lightweight than oak, has a rich pleasant colour, and polishes well. Besides furniture, walnut wood was widely taken up to make many other items such as carved or turned ornamental pieces, wall panelling, musical instruments, toys, picture frames, decorative veneer, and so forth. However, it was in the manufacture of gun stocks that walnut was most especially prized, and it was utilised for this at an impressive rate. It was estimated that 12,000 walnut trees were felled for this purpose alone in Europe in 1806. Many early nineteenth-century writers lamented the loss of walnut trees that resulted; an anonymous British author wrote just after the Napoleonic wars:

The demand for musket and pistol stocks during the late war thinned England of its walnut trees; and the deficiency should be made up by fresh planting. At that

Elderly walnut trees may become hollow with age, which weakens them; this one near Swindon was over 300 years old but collapsed in a storm in 2013.

period, the timber was so much in demand that a fine tree has often been sold for several hundred pounds.

In fact, walnut trees were not replanted in great numbers because the profits from growing walnut trees collapsed. It was often wisely said that a man who planted a walnut sapling would grow old and die before it became large enough to be useful, and the trees do take a long time to reach a mature size. Instead of waiting decades for British landowners to plant more walnut trees, gun manufacturers sought alternative sources of timber from abroad such as the black walnut from North America, or mahogany and other tropical woods. This has meant that large walnut trees are not a common sight in the UK any more, whereas in the seventeenth century John Evelyn noted many plantations of the tree in England, especially around Surrey.

Going nuts over a tree

Somerset's most famous tree was its Glastonbury Thorn – a type of hawthorn that was supposed to flower over Christmas. However, there was once another celebrated tree in the town, as described by eighteenth-century historian John Collinson:

> Besides the holy thorn, there grew in the abbey churchyard of Glastonbury, on the north side of St Joseph's Chapel, a miraculous walnut tree which never budded forth before the feast of St Barnabas (June 11); but on that very day shot forth leaves, and flourished like its usual species. This tree is gone, and in the place thereof stands a very fine walnut tree of the common sort. It is strange to say how much this tree was sought after by the credulous; and though not an uncommon walnut, Queen Anne, King James, and many of the nobility of the realm, even when the times of monkish superstition had ceased, gave large sums of money for small cuttings from the original.

Willow

Freshly cut willow timber.

*T*here are several species of willow that grow in the UK, and many varieties of them, some of which have well-established regional names such as osier, withy or sallow. Certain species, such as goat willow (*Salix caprea*), white willow (*S. alba*), crack willow (*S. fragilis*) and osier willow (*S. viminalis*) are native to the UK. Others are more recent introductions. The weeping willow, perhaps surprisingly given its prominence as a feature of many UK riversides, is not a native species and came originally from China. This is the tree shown in the famous blue-on-white 'willow pattern' china – a design that was heavily inspired by Chinese work but was largely created in its present form in England in the late eighteenth century.

The name 'weeping willow' is derived from a passage in Psalm 137 of the Bible where exiled Israelites sit down amongst trees by the river Euphrates in Babylon and weep because they miss their home country. Unfortunately, the wild species that was given the name of weeping willow, *Salix babylonica*, is not native to Babylon but the name has stuck.

The English poet Alexander Pope (1688–1744) is often credited with planting the first weeping willow in the UK. The story goes that Pope's friend, Lady Suffolk, received a woven basket of figs from abroad and he noticed that one of the basket twigs seemed about to sprout, so he planted it. This was claimed to have grown into a weeping willow. Unfortunately, this tale is almost certainly untrue: weeping willow is not used to make baskets and anyway, a twig is most unlikely to have survived the long sea journeys of

'Willow pattern' china, showing a stylised weeping willow tree growing to the right of the bridge.

Weeping willow.

the eighteenth century. Besides, other sources suggest that the weeping willow was first grown at Hampton Court in 1692. However, it is true that there was a famous weeping willow on Alexander Pope's estate. Nearly fifty years after his death the tree was living, though ailing, and still famous. A feature in the *New London Magazine* in 1789 explained:

> Towards the bottom of the slope, propped with uncommon care, and guarded by a holy zeal from the ravages of time, still stands the weeping willow planted by the hand of Pope. From this, a thousand slips [cuttings] are annually transmitted to the most distant quarters of the globe, and… happy is he who can get a small portion of it.

Pope's tree sired many others, but eventually died in 1801. Another famous weeping willow is associated with Napoleon. It is said that he took a particular liking to a young tree on the island of St Helena where he was held prisoner by the British, and even had a seat fixed under it. The original tree seems to have died not long after Napoleon's death in 1821, but it was replaced perhaps with a cutting from the original, and many further cuttings were taken and exported all over the world. In 1838, the botanist John Loudon describes the enduring British fascination with the French emperor:

> It has become fashionable to possess a plant of the true Napoleon's willow; and in consequence a great many cuttings have been imported, and a number of plants sold by the London nurserymen. There are now trees of it in a great many places.

Pencil drawing of willow trees growing on Napoleon's grave at St Helena in 1892. (*Courtesy of Wellcome Collection https://wellcomecollection.org*)

There is a handsome small one in the Horticultural Society's Garden; one at Kew; several at Messrs Loddiges'; some in the Twickenham Botanic Garden; one in the garden of Captain Stevens, Beaumont Square, Mile End; one in the garden of Mr Knight at Canonbury Place, Islington, brought over in 1824; one in the garden of No.2 Lee Place, Lewisham, Kent; one in the garden of No.1 Porchester terrace…

And so the list goes on. These trees were particularly popular in Britain, and many communities had their own 'Napoleon willow'. Another famous man with a tree connection was Samuel Johnson, who had a favourite willow that was planted at his family home in Lichfield by his father. This was a variety of the crack willow, and was well known because Johnson once remarked that the tree was the delight both of his early and of his waning life: he played beneath it as a child, and in his older years often took rest beneath its shade. It is said that he never failed to visit it whenever he returned to Lichfield. By 1781, this tree had a girth of over 15 feet, and by 1810 was over 21 feet, but sadly it suffered a number of episodes of serious damage shortly after this and eventually collapsed completely in 1829. Dr Johnson died in 1784, so fortunately he never witnessed the decline and demise of his beloved willow, but the tree was so famous that *The Gentleman's Magazine* carried a leading article about the tree the following year and recorded precise details of its size and appearance.

The trees commonly identified as weeping willows in the UK these days are actually various kinds of hybrid. Many willow hybrids arise naturally because native willow species in the UK can freely fertilise one other. Some hybrids, and varieties of them created by human intervention, have special properties favoured by craftworkers in a particular industry. For example, even today there are many tens of varieties of osier willow used within the basket-making industry. These trees require long, thin branches that do not break when woven into shape, and which do not rot quickly. The willows are regularly cut by coppicing so that the desirable branches are removed without killing the tree, and allowing further growth to replace them. Since prehistoric times, Britons have utilised willow in this way to make storage baskets and carrying containers. Like hazel, which was similarly harvested, willow branches were woven together to make the fence panels known as hurdles, and in the wattle and daub construction technique for buildings. For centuries, willow weaving was the principal means to

Dr Johnson's willow at Lichfield, shortly before its final collapse in 1829.

Victorian fishermen at Elie, Scotland (top), showing the customary baskets woven from willow and used for selling and transporting fish. Willow branches woven to make fence panels (bottom).

create the fishing pots needed to reap the harvest of the sea such as crabs and lobsters, and beehives were often woven in this manner as well.

The botanist John Knapp observed in 1829 that the heavy pruning of willows for timber and branches was so universal that it affected our whole view of the tree within the landscape of the UK:

> There is one race of trees, the willow, very common about us, that is so universally subject to this pollarding, for the purpose of providing stakes and hurdles for the farm, that probably few persons have ever seen a willow tree. At any rate, a sight of one grown unmutilated from the root is a rare occurrence. The few that I have seen constituted trees of great beauty.

However, the growing and management of willows was so popular in Cambridgeshire and the former neighbouring county of Huntingdonshire that the tree was known there as the 'Cambridge oak'. Willows grow very fast compared to other trees, hence willow plantations were a good business prospect. The historian Thomas Fuller recorded this popular local saying in 1662: 'the profit by willows will buy the owner a horse, before that by other trees will pay for his saddle.'

Willow coppicing encourages growth of many long narrow branches, which are regularly harvested for weaving.

The wood of the white willow was found to be particularly robust and disinclined to shatter when struck. In England it was the traditional material for cricket bats, mallets and other articles required to give or receive hard blows without splintering, such as the linings of carts that carried stones from quarries. However, as far as cricket is concerned, the modern bat is now made from a specific variety of white willow called the 'cricket bat willow' (*Salix alba* var. *caerulea*), which is still grown commercially in plantations for this reason. Yet, historically, willow wood was considered suitable for a whole range of other functions. John Evelyn offered a very long list of contemporary uses in 1664, including: boxes, gun stocks, clogs, forks and rakes, rafters, ladders, poles, lattices, platters, whetstones, buckets, and 'little casks and vessels'.

Willow was one of a number of trees sourced in the manufacture of charcoal, but was very extensively used for this purpose because the charcoal produced was held to be especially good quality, burning with a high heat. Charcoal was important to the iron and steel industry, as well as in the manufacture of gunpowder. In 1788, there were eighty-six iron furnaces in England, of which twenty-six were still fuelled by charcoal. By the nineteenth century, of course, all of these were fuelled by coal in the form of coke.

Despite the value of willow wood, in some parts of the country there was hostility to cutting down these trees for timber. In the Fens of eastern England, for example, many

Cricket bats are traditionally only made from willow.

builders and carpenters would avoid willow timber for domestic construction as it was said to be the wood often chosen for constructing the gallows, hence it would bring bad luck.

The willow seems to have been considered a funereal tree and an emblem of grief since remote times. In particular, it was associated with forsaken love or the death of a romantic relationship, and those affected might actually wear willow leaves as a badge of mourning. So universal was the link with sadness and grief, that 'to wear the willow' was once a familiar proverb. Accordingly, in the seventeenth century, Thomas Fuller described the willow as 'a sad tree, whereof such who have lost their love make their mourning garlands'. Depictions of the willow became symbolic of loss or bereavement, and a woman who grieved the death of a lover or husband was sometimes said to be 'in her willows'. An unknown author pokes fun at this practice in a satirical work published in 1723. The book was appropriately called *The Comical Pilgrim or Travels of a Cynick Philosopher Thro' the Most Wicked Parts of the World*, and some believe the author to have been Daniel Defoe:

> I went into Huntingdonshire, which is a very proper county for unsuccessful lovers; for upon the loss of their sweethearts they will here find an abundance of willow trees, so that they may either wear the willow green or hang themselves, which they please; but the latter is reckoned the best remedy for slighted love.

Depictions of the willow could represent mourning, and they may feature on gravestones.

An altogether more sinister belief about this tree in some parts of the country was that willows could uproot themselves at night and stalk the unwary traveller walking through the woods after dark.

In the absence of true palm leaves, leafy willow twigs and branches were often cut and displayed in churches or homes to celebrate Palm Sunday. They decorated the church, often strewn on pews to mimic the palm branches thrown before Christ when he entered Jerusalem on the back of a donkey. Perhaps because of this Christian association, willow twigs in the house were thought to bring good luck. The fluffy catkins of some species are known as pussy willow, because of their supposed resemblance to a little cat, but in the past they were also called 'goslings' for the same reason.

Nicholas Culpeper notes the many and varied uses of willow medicinally. Practitioners used it to treat everything from bleeding to wind, and even lust. Water gathered from the willow when it flowered was rated as a good treatment for poor sight and skin spots. The burnt ashes of the bark mixed with vinegar was recommended to take away 'warts, corns, and superfluous flesh'. Culpeper goes on to add that 'It is a fine cool tree, the boughs of which are very convenient to be placed in the chamber of one sick of a fever.' And physicians actually did this: they noted the cool shade under a willow tree and so

Is there a willow following you? Some believed the tree could uproot and walk about at night. This particular 'stalker' is made by cleverly weaving a living willow into a human shape.

advised taking branches indoors to hang above the bed of someone with a temperature in the belief that it would cool them.

A related ancient role for willow was to make a drink from the bark for treating fever and rheumatism, or to chew it to treat pain. These properties were known to many ancient civilisations including the Greeks and the Romans, and have some foundation in science. Willow contains salicylic acid, which was the basis for the modern synthesis of aspirin, used medicinally to treat pain, fever and inflammation just as willow bark was. Concentrated salicylic acid itself is still employed medicinally as a solution applied to the skin for one of the roles recommended by Culpeper: to remove warts and corns.

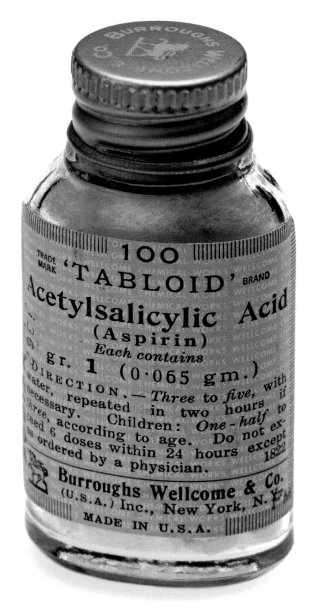

Aspirin is derived from salicylic acid, a natural painkiller and anti-inflammatory found in willow bark. (*Courtesy of Wellcome Collection https://wellcomecollection.org*)

Yew

Yew topiary.

*T*he yew has an ancient name, being *íw* or *éow* in Old English. It has a very longstanding connection with death and mourning, although how yews came to be so frequently associated with churches and graveyards is uncertain. In 1658, Sir Thomas Browne wrote:

> Whether the planting of yew in churchyards hold not its original from ancient funeral rites, or as an emblem of resurrection from its perpetual verdure, may also admit conjecture.

It is known that early Christian churches were often built on sites that had been revered by pagan religions. Some ancient yews are older than the churches they stand next to, so it may be that pre-Christian religions held the yew in special reverence. As Browne suggests, the fact that these trees stay green throughout the winter may mean that they were once symbolic of the 'return to life' that happened every spring and so were a metaphor for immortality or the afterlife.

Alternatively, since the yew has been linked with death in several ancient cultures, the association may have been brought to Britannia by the Romans. Pliny, for example, pronounced that the yew had a 'sombre and ominous aspect', and Ovid wrote that the pathway to the underworld and its associated river Styx was lined with yew trees:

> *A shelving path in shadows of sad yew*
> *through utter silence to the deep descends,*
> *infernal, where the languid Styx exhales vapours;*
> *and there the shadows of the dead descend,*
> *after they leave their sacred urns.*

The seventeenth-century herbalist Robert Turner offers a different reason for yew trees being planted near to churches, at a time when 'bad smells' were thought to cause serious disease:

> The yew is hot and dry, having such attraction that if planted near a place subject to poisonous vapours, its very branches will draw and imbibe them. For this reason it was planted in churchyards, and commonly on the west side, which was at one time considered full of putrefaction and gross oleaginous gasses exhaled from the graves by the setting sun. These gasses, or will-o'-the-wisps, diverse [persons] have seen, and believed them dead bodies walking abroad. Wheresoever it grows it is both dangerous and deadly to man and beast; the very lying under its branches has been found hurtful, yet the growing of it in churchyards is useful.

It was formerly a custom to carry branches of yew at funerals and on other sorrowful occasions, and to place them in graves with the dead. Shakespeare, for example, writes of a 'shroud of white, stuck all with yew'. Eighteenth-century British poet Robert Blair

Five hundred-year-old yew at the Church of St Mary the Virgin, Twyford, Hampshire. It is reputedly the oldest clipped yew in the UK.

captured perfectly the funereal associations between the yew and the cemetery in his verses called, appropriately enough, *The Grave*. In the lines below, he describes one unmistakable method to recognise a graveyard:

> *Well do I know thee by thy trusty yew,*
> *Cheerless, unsocial plant, that loves to dwell*
> *'Midst skulls and coffins, epitaphs, and worms;*
> *Where light-heeled ghosts, and visionary shades,*
> *Beneath the wan cold moon (so fame reports),*
> *Embodied, thick, perform their mystic rounds.*
> *No other merriment, dull tree, is thine.*

The story even arose that yew trees fed upon the remains of the dead. This is something that we now know to be biologically correct, albeit indirectly. When flesh decays it returns to basic chemicals that nourish the soil and the plants that grow within it. However, the mere concept of a plant feeding on dead people was considered horrific and macabre by our ancestors, and it lent the yew a sinister reputation. Reports of yew roots being found invading disinterred coffins only added fuel to the fire. Tennyson refers to this ghoulish inclination of the yew in his poem *In Memoriam*:

> *Old yew, which graspest at the stones*
> *That name the underlying dead,*
> *Thy fibres net the dreamless head,*
> *Thy roots are wrapt about the bones.*

Given all the magic and mysticism associated with the yew, and its great longevity, it is no surprise that many individual trees have acquired a certain celebrity. Britain's yews are amongst the most ancient trees in Europe, but arriving at an accurate date for living specimens is very difficult because they tend to become hollow and sometimes their trunks divide, so that counting tree rings is not possible even in dead trees. One of the oldest – perhaps *the* oldest – is the Fortingall Yew in Perthshire, Scotland, which may be as much as 5,000 years old, but there are many ancient yews in churchyards in Wales that may be as old, or older. Celebrated elderly yews in England include the Tisbury Yew in Wiltshire and the Linton Yew in Herefordshire. Bizarrely, there are two ancient yews known as the Crowhurst Yew, both in villages of this name: one in East Sussex and one in neighbouring Surrey. Coincidentally, each yew grows in a graveyard attached to a St George's Church, and both are probably over 1,500 years old.

As already noted, some yew trees become hollow with age. The resultant space in the Tisbury Yew could hold up to nine people, but it was filled in with concrete in the 1940s in an attempt to strengthen the tree. The hollow of the Crowhurst Yew in Surrey was enlarged in the early nineteenth century and once allowed twelve people to sit inside for tea – a door was fitted, which can still be seen, although it is now wedged

This ancient contorted yew at Crowhurst, East Sussex, is of uncertain age but may be about 1,500 years old. It was certainly a mature tree in 1066 when the Battle of Hastings raged about 4 miles away.

Rock-a-bye baby

A yew tree is behind one theory for the origin of the nursey rhyme *Rock-a-bye Baby*, which has these lyrics:

> *Rock-a-bye baby on the treetop,*
> *When the wind blows, the cradle will rock,*
> *When the bough breaks, the cradle will fall,*
> *And down will come baby: cradle and all.*

In the eighteenth century, Betty Kenny and her husband, a charcoal maker, lived in a very large hollow yew tree in Shining Cliff Woods, Derbyshire. They had many children, became well known for their unusual lifestyle, and supposedly used a hollowed-out branch of the tree as a cradle, which led ultimately to the nursery rhyme, so it is said. A few sparse, decayed remains of the 'Betty Kenny Tree' can still be seen, although it probably died over a century ago.

shut. Even today, the Much Marcle Yew in Herefordshire holds a seat that can take up to eight people.

Henry VIII is supposed to have wooed Anne Boleyn under the spreading branches of a yew at Ankerwycke, an island on the river Thames not far from his palace at Windsor. The tree is still standing. Another famous yew, which has not been so fortunate, has become known as the Selborne Yew. This was a great favourite of the eighteenth-century naturalist Gilbert White, and for many years it had a ring-shaped seat running around it. White measured the circumference of the trunk in 1789 and reported it at nearly 23 feet. Sadly, the tree was blown down in 1990. A local campaign led to the trunk being re-erected shortly afterwards, since many of the roots were still intact, but to no avail.

The yew has been a popular subject for topiary in the UK, something that was particularly in vogue in the sixteenth century. Yews are clipped into geometric shapes or made to resemble giant birds or other animals. The yew at the Church of St Mary the Virgin, Twyford, Hampshire lays claim to being the oldest regularly clipped yew in the UK, even though the tree is probably only about 500 years old. It is cut into a large dome shape. Yew was also grown as a high impenetrable hedge to divide gardens, act as a windbreak, or to prevent entry to properties.

The yew has been hailed as highly poisonous since antiquity. Pliny described beliefs about its toxicity in the first century:

> In the male tree the fruit is injurious; indeed, in Spain more particularly, the berries contain a deadly poison. It is an ascertained fact that travellers' vessels, made in Gaul of this wood, for the purpose of holding wine, have caused the death of those who used them. Sextius says, that in Greece this tree is known by the name of 'smilax', and that in Arcadia it is possessed of so active a poison, that those who sleep beneath it, or even take food there, are sure to meet their death from it.

The Selborne Yew when it was alive in about 1905 (above). The contemporary caption says: '1200 years old, girth 27 feet 9 inches'. The dead husk of the main trunk in 2017 (below), topped with red-berried honeysuckle.

The red fruits of the yew are often known as 'berries', but are in fact a fleshy coating around the seed known as an aril. Birds eat the fruits and swallow the seeds, which are later dispersed in their faeces.

Pliny will have known about celebrated cases where the yew was supposedly taken as poison. For example, in the account of his military conquests, Julius Caesar wrote that one Gaulish chieftain called Cativolcus, when faced with defeat, 'destroyed himself with the juice of the yew-tree'. Other ancient writers supported Pliny's assertion that all parts of the tree were toxic and that it was dangerous to lie beneath it. However, Tudor herbalist John Gerard was perhaps the first to rebut these ideas:

> Dioscorides writeth, and generally all that heretofore have dealt in the faculty of herbs, that the yew tree is very venomous to be taken inwardly, and that if any do sleep under the shadow thereof it causeth sickness and oftentimes death. Moreover they say that the fruit thereof being eaten is not only dangerous and deadly unto man, but if birds eat thereof it causeth them to cast their feathers and many times to die. All which I boldly affirm is altogether untrue: for when I was young and went to school, diverse of my school-fellows, and likewise myself, did eat our fills of the berries of this tree, and have not only slept under the shadow thereof, but among the branches also, without any hurt at all, and that not one time but many times.

English archer from a thirteenth-century bestiary with a bow that may have been made from yew. (*Courtesy of the British Library illuminated manuscripts collection www.bl.uk*)

The yew's association with death extended to the principal use of its timber. Yew wood is pliant and tough, and in the medieval period it was the preferred wood for making the bows of English archers. In the skilled hands of well-trained practitioners, longbows made from yew were powerful weapons that played a vital part in English victories against the French at battles in the Hundred Years' War such as Crécy, Poitiers, and Agincourt. Seventeenth-century pastoral poet William Browne wrote:

> *The warlike yew by which, more than the lance,*
> *The strong-armed English spirits conquered France.*

The earliest surviving book about English archery is *Toxophilus* by Roger Ascham, written in 1545 and dedicated to Henry VIII. In it, Ascham expounds the virtue of yew as the first choice for making bows:

> As for brazil wood, elm, wych, and ash, experience doth prove them to be but mean for bows, and so to conclude yew of all other things is that whereof perfect shooting would have a bow made.
>
> This wood as it is now general and common among Englishmen, so hath it continued for a long time and had the most praise for bows, [even] among the Romans as doth appear in this half verse of Virgil: *taxi torquentiir in aretes* ('yew fit for a bow to be made').
>
> [Text substantially modernised]

As a consequence of this pre-eminence, large quantities of yew were imported from the rest of Europe. Archery was considered such a vital national skill that a law passed by Henry VIII declared that all subjects under sixty years of age 'not lame, decrepit or maimed, or having any other lawful impediment' were to regularly practise with the longbow. Parents had to provide every boy aged seven to seventeen with a bow and two arrows, and practice ranges with targets had to be available in every town. Shakespeare writes in his play *Richard II* of those who 'learn to bend their bows, Of double-fatal yew'. The yew was double-fatal because it not only provided the bow, it was poisonous too.

Our most distant ancestors used the yew to make other weapons as well. In 1911, the top of a wooden spear was found at Clacton-on-Sea. It is made of yew, is over 400,000 years old, and is the oldest known worked wooden implement in the world.

Interestingly, although the yew has a longstanding association with death, chemicals found in the tree have helped to save lives in modern times. The Latin name for the yew tree is *taxus*, and a series of cancer medicines called taxanes now exist: all based upon the structure of compounds isolated from yew trees. The two most well known are paclitaxel (launched in 1994 with the brandname 'Taxol') and docetaxel (brandname 'Taxotere'). Taxanes were originally found by US scientists in a different species of yew to the one found in the UK, called the Pacific yew, but they occur in the European yew as well.

Index

alcoholic beverages, 11, 41–3, 49, 138, 175
alder, 1–5
Apollo, 24–5
apple, 6–14
archery, 21, 151, 153, 161, 200–201
ash, 15–22
ash, mountain (*see* rowan)

Banks, Joseph, 43, 109
bay, 23–9
beech, 30–7
birch, 38–43
birdlime, 82
boats (*see* shipbuilding)
Boleyn, Ann, 58
builder's timber, 145
Byron, Lord, 53–5

Caesar, Gaius Julius, 26, 199
Carlyle, Thomas, 17
carver's tree, 97
charcoal, 5, 73, 88, 168, 188, 197
Charles II, 125, 133
cherry, 44–51
Christian church, 9, 40, 45–6, 64–5, 69, 80, 83, 97, 130, 152, 159, 170, 180, 182, 190, 193
Christmas, 64–5, 80–1, 142, 152, 180
Claudius, emperor, 26
Compton, Henry, 108–109
Cowley, Abraham, 75
Culpeper, Nicholas, 5, 13–14, 17–18, 26–7, 36, 59, 68, 77, 100, 117, 138, 153, 166, 171, 190–91

divining, 75–6
dyes, 2, 40, 179

Elizabeth I, 53, 126
elm, 52–61

Evelyn, John, 2, 21, 32–5, 39, 59, 75–6, 80, 88, 97–8, 114–15, 140, 146, 153, 159–60, 165–6, 173, 180, 188
execution (*see* hangings)

Gay, John, 75
George III, 25, 128
Gerard, John, 2, 5, 13, 17, 21, 59, 76, 82, 86, 100, 117, 133, 137–8, 152, 172, 177, 199
Gibbons, Grinling, 97
Gilpin, William, 98, 113
Glyndŵr, Owain, 129
Gray, Thomas, 31
Greeks, ancient, 9, 16, 18, 24–7, 33, 146, 149–50, 163, 177, 191

hangings, 56–7, 129, 171–2
hawthorn, 62–70
hazel, 71–7
hedges, 68–9, 79–80, 87–8, 113, 136, 197
Henry VII, 65
Henry VIII, 53, 129, 197, 200–201
Herrick, Robert, 46, 49, 166
Hill, Aaron, 36
holly, 78–84
Hood, Robin, 125, 151, 175
hornbeam, 85–90
horse chestnut, 91–4
husbandman's tree, 21

ink, 2, 133–4, 179

Johnson, Samuel, 185
Joseph of Arimathea, 64–5
Jupiter, 166, 177

Lauder, Thomas, 143, 171
lime, 95–101
Linnaeus, Carl, 100

London plane, 102–106
Loudon, John Claudius, 29, 40, 86–7, 98, 155, 165, 170, 173–4, 184–5

magnolia, 107–11
maple, 112–17
Mary Queen of Scots, 65
Merlin, 63, 129
monkey puzzle, 118–22
Morris, William, 89–90

Napoleon, 25, 111, 184
Newton, Isaac, 9
Nicol, Walter, 40, 79, 98, 143, 154
Norse mythology, 16–17, 158

oak, 18, 123–34
Ovid, 24, 37, 193

pear, 135–40
Pechey, John, 41, 50, 84, 101, 146, 153, 166
pine 141–7
Pliny, 17, 25, 35, 47–8, 81, 117, 136, 163, 193, 197–9
Pope, Alexander, 182–4
poplar, 148–55

Richard III, 65
Romans, 3, 21, 24–6, 31, 35–6, 39, 47–8, 76, 81, 96, 136, 146, 152, 162–3, 177–9, 193
rowan, 156–61

Scotland, 3, 5, 17, 40, 56–7, 63, 65, 129, 137, 142–5, 158, 160, 171–2, 175, 186, 195

Shakespeare, William, 26, 37, 65–6, 67, 129, 137, 152, 172, 193, 201
shipbuilding, 3, 33, 119, 130–2, 145–6, 159
Smith, James, 35
Standish, Arthur, 68
sweet chestnut, 162–8
sycamore, 169–75

Tennyson, Alfred, 152, 195
Tiberius, emperor, 25–6
Tolpuddle Martyrs, 175
Tradescant, John the Younger, 103
Turing, Alan, 9–11
Turner, Robert, 193
Turner, William, 40, 158

Venice, 3
Victoria, Queen, 55–6
Vindolanda tablets, 39

Wales, 39, 124, 129, 149, 159–60, 195
Wallace, William, 56–7, 129
walnut, 176–180
Washington, George, 45
Wesley, John, 22, 53
White, Gilbert, 167, 197–8
William II, 125–6
willow, 181–91
Woolf, Virginia, 61

yew, 192–201

Zeus, 9, 16, 150